Critical Edition of the Complete Works

of

Saint Thérèse of the Child Jesus and of the Holy Face

Centenary Edition
(1873–1973)

The Prayers
of
Saint Thérèse of Lisieux

The Act of Oblation

General Introduction by Guy Gaucher, O.C.D.

Translated by Aletheia Kane, O.C.D.

ICS Publications
Institute of Carmelite Studies
Washington, DC
1997

This edition was prepared by Sister Cécile of the Carmel of Lisieux and Mgr Guy Gaucher, O.C.D., auxiliary bishop of Bayeux and Lisieux, with the assistance of Père Bernard Bro, O.P., and Jeanne and Jacques Lonchampt.

PRAYERS OF ST. THÉRÈSE OF LISIEUX: THE ACT OF OBLA-TION is a translation of *Prières: l'offrande à l'Amour Miséricordieux* (Paris: Les Éditions du Cerf / Desclée de Brouwer, 1988). Photos used with permission of Office Central de Lisieux.

Cover design by Nancy Gurganus of Grey Coat Graphics.

ICS Publications
2131 Lincoln Road, N.E.
Washington, D.C. 20002
202-832-8489

Library of Congress Cataloging-in-Publication Data

Thérèse, de Lisieux, Saint, 1873–1897.
   [Prières. English]
   The Prayers of Saint Thérèse of Lisieux : the act of oblation /
preface by Guy Gaucher ; translated by Aletheia Kane. —
Centenary ed. (1873–1973)
   p. cm. — (Critical edition of the complete works [texts and words] of Saint Thérèse of the Child Jesus and of the Holy Face)
Includes bibliographical references and index.
Contents: [1] Texts and introductions.
ISBN 0-935216-60-X
   1. Catholic Church— Prayer-books and devotions—English.
2. Thérèse, de Lisieux, Saint, 1873–1897. Prières. I. Gaucher, Guy, 1930– . II. Kane, Aletheia. III. Title. IV. Series: Thérèse, de Lisieux, Saint, 1873–1897. Works. English. 1982.
BX2179.T5P7513 1997
242'.802—dc21   96–50347
                                   CIP

Contents

Editor's Preface

In the years immediately after her death, Thérèse's writings circulated only in highly edited excerpts. As her popularity grew, however, so too did the demand for more of her works, in better editions. To meet this need, teams of Theresian scholars labored for decades to bring out critical editions of her texts in successive volumes, a task only recently completed in the eight-volume "Nouvelle Édition du Centenaire" (Paris: Cerf/DDB, 1992).

For nearly as many years, following the lead of the late John Clarke, O.C.D., the Institute of Carmelite Studies has worked to translate these same critical editions, so that contemporary readers in the English-speaking world may come to know and love the authentic voice of Thérèse, without the "improvements" pious editors had imposed on her writings. The present book, together with the long-anticipated volume of Thérèse's plays, will finally bring Father John's dream to fulfillment.

Thérèse of Lisieux was a woman of deep prayer, in a religious community dedicated to praying. We should not be surprised, then, to find numerous prayers scattered throughout her writings. But besides those contained in her autobiography, letters, poetry, and plays, Thérèse left behind 21 independent prayers, of differing tone and length, written for varied persons and occasions.

The present volume brings these prayers together for the first time, with ample commentary to illuminate their context and meaning. Here we find prayers to the Infant Jesus and Holy Face, prayers to Mary and the saints, prayers composed in joy and sorrow, prayers written for her novices and missionary brothers. Though few in number, they contain the full message of Thérèse in miniature, and include some of the most important texts she ever composed, such as her "Profession Note," the "Consecration to the Holy Face," and the "Oblation to Merciful Love."

In contrast to previous volumes of the Saint's writings from ICS Publications, for the *Prayers* we have kept more of the critical apparatus from the French edition. This means that the brief text of each prayer is followed by detailed information on the autographs and circumstances of composition, as well as a line-by-line commentary on Thérèse's sources, parallel passages, and the meaning of her words. Here readers will find, for example, the first critical edition of the famed "Oblation to Merciful Love," with an analysis of the different drafts of this precious text.

For easier cross-referencing, we have retained the French enumeration of the prayers (*prières*), here labeled Pri 1 to Pri 21. Notes for each are tagged to the line numbers in the original manuscripts, which are here indicated by superscripts in the text of the translated prayers; "recto" [r] and "verso" [v] refer to the front and back of the same manuscript sheet. For quotations from Teresa of Avila, John of the Cross, and Thérèse herself, we have used existing translations from ICS Publications. We have also used existing translations of other cited works whenever possible.

Sr. Aletheia Kane, O.C.D., carefully weighed various options in translating this work. For the sake of consistency, she incorporated John Clarke's earlier translations of Thérèse's "Profession Note" and "Oblation to Merciful Love" as they appear in our edition of *Story of a Soul,* changing only the capitalization and punctuation to conform to the current French edition. Elsewhere as well Thérèse's distinctive use of majuscules, points of suspension, and so on, were retained from the French. Occasionally a slightly awkward English expression was needed to preserve an important distinction in the French. Thus in Pri 4 and 10 "réparer" is translated "to repair for" rather than "to make reparation for," since the actual word "reparation" appears only twice (Pri 7 and LT 108) in all of Thérèse's writings; as the notes emphasize, hers was not primarily a spirituality of "reparation" in the usual sense.

The translator wishes to thank Sr. Mary Magdalen Kelly, O.C.D., of the Little Rock Carmel and Prof. Kathryn Wildgen, Ph.D., chair of the French Department at the University of New Orleans, for reading and commenting upon various drafts of her work. Thanks are also due to Jude Langsam for her editing and layout of the book. Our hope is that readers may use it not only to study Thérèse's prayers, but to pray *with* Thérèse herself.

Steven Payne, OCD
Editor, ICS Publications

Abbreviations

Pri 1, 2, etc.   Enumeration of the twenty-one prayers included in the French and English language editions of the present work.

The following abbreviations refer to other translations available from ICS Publications. The first four were translated by John Clarke, O.C.D.:

SS	*Story of a Soul,* 3d ed. (1976, 1996)
HLC	*Her Last Conversations* (1977)
GCI	*Letters of St. Thérèse of Lisieux, vol. I* (1982)
GCII	*Letters of St. Thérèse of Lisieux, vol. II* (1988)
PST	*The Poetry of Saint Thérèse of Lisieux,* translated by Donald Kinney, O.C.D. (1996)

Other abbreviations used in the volume include:

ACL	Archives of the Carmel of Lisieux.
Afd	Autograph, double sheet (*feuillet double*).
Afs	Autograph, single sheet (*feuillet simple*).
AL	*Annales de sainte Thérèse de Liseux* (journal).
BT	*La Bible avec Thérèse de Lisieux* (Paris: Cerf / DDB, 1979).
CDT	Center of Theresian documentation (Carmel of Lisieux).
CE I, etc.	Copie des Écrits [Copy of the Writings], 1910 (CE I, II, III, IV).
CG I, II	*Correspondance générale de Thérèse de Lisieux,* 1972–1973, 2 volumes.
CJ	"Carnet jaune" ["Yellow Notebook"] of Mother Agnes of Jesus.

CMG I, etc.	Manuscript notebooks of Sister Geneviève (CMG I to IV).
CRM	"Carnet rouge" ["Red Notebook"] of Sister Marie of the Trinity; cf. VT, no. 74–75, April–May 1979.
CSG	*Conseils et souvenirs,* publiés par soeur Geneviève, "Foi vivante," 1973. (Cf. *Memoir.*)
CSM	*Conseils et souvenirs relatés par soeur Marie de la Trinity* and published in VT 73 and 77. [A memoir by Sister Marie of the Trinity].
CV	Cinq Cahiers verts de Mère Agnès de Jésus, 1909, publiés en DE II. [The Five Green Notebooks of Mother Agnes of Jesus, published in DE II].
DCL	Documentation of the Carmel of Lisieux.
DE	*Derniers Entretiens* [*Last Conversations*], 1971.
DE II	Volume of Appendices to *Derniers Entretiens,* 1971.
HA 98, etc.	*Histoire d'une âme,* 1898 edition (07 = 1907, etc.).
Im	*Imitation of Christ.*
K-RJ	*Collected Works of St. John of the Cross,* translated by Kieran Kavanaugh, O.C.D. and Otilio Rodriguez, O.C.D., rev. ed., (Washington, DC: ICS Publications, 1991)
LC	Letters of Thérèse's correspondents (in CG and GC).
LT	Thérèse's letters (in CG and GC).
Memoir	*A Memoir of my Sister St. Thérèse,* by Sister Geneviève of the Holy Face, translated by the Carmelite Sisters of New York (New York: P. J. Kenedy and Sons, 1959). (Translation of earlier edition of CSG.)
Ms A	Manuscrit autobiographique [autobiographical manuscript] dedicated to Mother Agnes of Jesus (1895).
Ms B	Manuscrit autobiographique [autobiographical manuscript], letter to Sister Marie of the Sacred Heart (1896).
Ms C	Manuscrit autobiographique [autobiographical manuscript] dedicated to Mother Marie de Gonzague (1897).

Mss I, etc.	Three volumes of P. François de Sainte-Marie, accompanying the facsimile edition (1956) of the *Manuscrits autobiographiques* (Mss I, II, III).
Mes Armes	*Mes Armes* (Paris: Cerf/DDB, 1975). Cf. PN 48.
NPPO	Notes préparatoires pour le Procès de l'Ordinaire [Preparatory notes for the Ordinary Process].
NV	*Novissima Verba* (1927).
PA	Procès apostolique [Apostolic Process], 1915–1917 (Rome, 1976).
PN	Poésies de Thérèse. New numbering of the Centenary Edition, 1979. (Original French edition of PST above).
PO	Procès de l'Ordinaire [Ordinary Process], 1910–1911 (Rome, 1973).
RP	*Théâtre au Carmel: Récréations pieuses* de Sainte Thérèse de l'Enfant Jésus, 1985.
RP 1, etc.	The eight Pious Recreations (RP 1, 2, etc.).
TH	*Le Triomphe de l'Humilité (RP 7)* (Paris: Cerf/DDB, 1975).
VT	*Vie thérésienne*, Lisieux (quarterly review)
VTL	*Visage de Thérèse de Lisieux* (1961), in two volumes. Translated by Peter-Thomas Rohrbach, under the title *The Photo Album of St. Thérèse of Lisieux* (New York: P. J. Kenedy & Sons, 1962).

General Introduction

GUY GAUCHER, O.C.D.
AUXILIARY BISHOP OF BAYEUX AND LISIEUX

Although Sister Thérèse wrote the twenty-one prayers that are gathered together in this volume, she was never tempted to the intense creativity of her era in this field. She even admitted that she didn't care very much for this abundant production:

> Outside the *Divine Office,* which I am very unworthy to recite, I do not have the courage to force myself to search out *beautiful* prayers in books. There are so many of them it really gives me a headache! and each prayer is more beautiful than the others! I cannot recite them all and, not knowing which to choose, I do like children who do not know how to read, I say very simply to God what I wish to tell him, without composing beautiful sentences, and He always understands me.[1]

These lines reveal Sister Thérèse's customary humor, although she is quite ill at the time she writes her last manuscript in June 1897. As far as she is concerned, she never wanted to write "beautiful" prayers; she is too simple, too childlike, too "little" since she discovered the way of confidence and love. In her eyes all that counts is the truth. Watch out for "false currency" in spiritual matters.[2] Always perceptive, the young Carmelite fears excessive wordiness: "I do not hold in contempt beautiful thoughts that nourish the soul and unite it with God; but for a long time I have understood

---

[1] Ms C, 25r.

[2] CJ 8.7.16 [HLC, p. 82].

that we must not depend on them and even make perfection con-
sist in receiving many spiritual lights. The most beautiful thoughts
are nothing without good works." [3]

As for herself, she prays very simply: "God does not weary of
hearing me even when I tell Him simply my pains and joys as if He
did not know them." [4]

As we have often said, she wrote out of obedience and not to
compose a literary work.[5] She fully subscribed to Mother Marie de
Gonzague's reflection that it is "not through letters Carmelites
must save souls but through prayer." [6]

All that flows from the heart and pen of Sr. Thérèse of the
Child Jesus expresses the same interior authenticity. The only "definition" she gave emphasizes this spontaneity: "For me, *prayer* is an
aspiration of the heart, it is a simple glance directed to Heaven, it
is a cry of gratitude and love in the midst of trial as well as joy; it is
something great, supernatural, which expands my soul and unites
me with Jesus." [7]

Obviously, the twenty-one prayers included here must not
make us forget all those that we find in her other writings. In the
autobiographical manuscripts contained in *Story of a Soul,* her account often slips into prayer. As she reads over her life from a
distance, the author is caught up in what she is recalling and

---

[3] Ms C, 19v.

[4] Ms C, 32v. Already, on the simplicity of her prayer at the end of 1893:
"When I am before the Tabernacle, I can say only one thing to our
Lord: My God, you know that I love you. And I feel that my prayer does
not tire Jesus; knowing the helplessness of His poor little spouse, He is
content with her good will" (LT 152). Thérèse often described her
prayers as "poor" (LT 99, 131, 198, 218) and "weak" (LT 159, 166).

[5] Ms C, 6r, 18v, 33r.

[6] Ms C, 24v.

[7] Ms C, 25r. We can compare this with the definition she knew by heart:
"Prayer is an elevation of our soul to God, to render Him our religious
due and to ask him for our needs" (*Catéchisme á l'usage du diocèse de
Bayeux* [Catechism for the diocese of Bayeux] presented by Bishop
Hugonin [Bayeux, 1882], p. 176).

spontaneously addresses Jesus. Then, coming to herself, she takes up again the thread of her account. For example: "What I am writing, dear Mother, has no continuity; my little story that resembled a fairy tale is all of a sudden changed into a prayer." [8]

On the level of writing, Thérèse reaches the heights when she speaks directly to Jesus, as in Manuscript B (September 1896): "When writing these words, I shall address them to Jesus since this makes it easier for me to express my thoughts." [9] The too-one-sided critiques about the poverty or sentimentality of her style collapse of themselves. The style here is that of the Carmelite consumed with love who converses with her Beloved. Carried away by her interior transport, she is brought up against the limits of language and often regrets that she can not truly express what she is experiencing: "Ah! I wish I could explain what I feel!" [10] —"It is quite impossible for the human tongue to express things that the human heart can hardly understand." [11] Having reached the boundaries of the ineffable,[12] Thérèse then lapses into silent, wordless prayer: "Frequently, only silence can express my prayer; however, this Divine Guest of the Tabernacle understands all, even the silence of a child's soul filled with gratitude!" [13]

We can gauge here the primary importance of the two hours of prayer in Sister Thérèse's Carmelite life. We need only reread

---

[8] Ms C, 6r; Cf. Ms A, 25; 84r; Ms C, 3r; 9v; 16r; 34r–v; 35r.

[9] Ms B, 1v.

[10] Ms A, 38v.

[11] Ms B, 1r.

[12] Père François de Sainte-Marie, *L'ineffable chez sainte Thérèse de l'Énfant Jésus* [The ineffable in St. Thérèse of the Child Jesus], Carmel, 1957, pp. 253–265.

[13] LT 138; LT 106. "On entering Thérèse's cell one day, I was struck by her heavenly expression of recollection. Although she was sewing industriously, she seemed lost in profound contemplation: When I inquired, 'What are you thinking about?' she replied with tears in her eyes: 'I am meditating on the *Our Father*. It is so sweet to call God our Father!' (CSG, p. 81; *Memoir*, p. 109).

the parable of the "little bird" (Manuscript B) to grasp very concretely Thérèse's attitude as she remains "gazing on her Divine Sun" whatever the clouds and storms.[14]

Moreover, is it not extremely revealing that of her fifty-four poems, thirty-three are prayers?[15] The pious recreations are strewn with them too.[16] The letters contain frequent exclamations to Jesus and biblical quotations. Often Thérèse assures her correspondents of her prayer for them and asks them to pray for her.[17]

Thérèse's Prayers

Thérèse left us twenty-one written prayers, very unequal in length, since some are no more than a line and the longest has 65 lines.

Without too much artificiality, we can group them according to rather easily discernible criteria:

- spontaneous prayers written in distress or in joy (Pri 1, 14–17, 19, 21);
- "pedagogical" prayers composed for the novices (Pri 3–5, 7, 18, 20) and one for a layperson (Pri 10);
- major prayers at decisive moments in Thérèse's life (Profession, Pri 2; Act of Oblation, Pri 6; prayer for a spiritual brother, Pri 8; consecration to the Holy Face, Pri 12).

Let us analyze these three categories of texts each in its turn, bearing in mind that each in its own way marks Thérèse's path as she begins to "run as a giant."[18]

---

[14] Ms B, 5r.

[15] Twenty-one address Jesus and God; five are to Mary; four to the saints; one to the angels; two to her family (one to her father, one to her deceased brothers and sisters).

[16] RP 1: prayer of Joan of Arc, p. 80; RP 2: prayer of the Angels at the crib, pp. 91ff [Page numbers for RP are to the French edition.–Trans.]; RP 3: prayers of Joan of Arc, pp. 128, 137, 150; RP 4: dialogues among Jesus, Martha, and Mary; RP 8: prayer of Saint Stanislas Kostka to Mary, pp. 282–285.

[17] Refer to the Index of CG II, p. 1379; consult the Concordance at CDT.

[18] Ms A, 45r, quoting Ps 18[19]:5.

Do not measure their importance by their length. What could be more poignant than these "prayer-exclamations" (Pri 1, 11, 19), these ejaculatory prayers, as they were called in her day; these arrows shot toward heaven, in the words of the Desert Fathers? They must have welled up from the depths of a distressed heart for Thérèse to wish to write them down so to reread and repeat them.

Her entreaty to the Virgin Mary (Pri 1) who had smiled on her "at the morning of her life," [19] on May 13, 1883, no doubt echoes those two "spiritual trials" [20] that will endure long after her physical healing.

Thirteen years later, written in greater anguish, Prayer 19 (1897) illustrates a passage from Manuscript C: "I believe I have made more acts of faith in this one year than during my whole life." [21] These two lines on a pitiful scrap of paper, testifying to the extreme harshness of her interior struggle, are more eloquent than a long discourse.

Shorter still, Prayer 11, inscribed above a tiny icon of the Holy Face, expresses her intense desire to resemble the Beloved announced by Isaiah 53.

In her dialogue with Jesus, Thérèse the Carmelite prays for the grace of likeness, in accordance with the desire of her teacher St. John of the Cross: to become like the Spouse of the *Canticle of Canticles*.[22] She manifests this desire again in Prayer 16: "Deign to imprint in me your divine likeness."

The prayers from the years 1893–1894 seem less fraught with a passion of anguish and impetuous love. We could describe them as "pedagogical," provided we don't think Thérèse wrote them only for another's use.

---

[19] PN 54.25.3.

[20] Ms A, 30v.

[21] Among these pathos-filled acts of faith made during her trial we recall the Creed written with her blood (Mother Agnes in PA, 151) and the inscription engraved in her cell: "Jesus is my only love."

[22] *Spiritual Canticle*, explanation of st. 36, p. 62 of Thérèse's copy [K-RJ 547].

Certainly she wanted to help the novices who had been entrusted to her (Sisters Martha, Marie-Madeleine of the Blessed Sacrament, Geneviève of St. Thérèse), but when she says "we" or "us" she wholeheartedly includes herself.

When she takes charge of her little flock, she draws them with her into an ascetic effort of reparation (Pri 6.9), especially against blasphemies (Pri 4). They are to keep custody of the eyes in the refectory (Pri 3), to be formed in prayer and sacrifices (Pri 5),[23] "to make the nightly examination of conscience" (Pri 7), and to acquire humility (Pri 20).[24]

It is probably no coincidence that Prayers 11 to 16 (1896 and the beginning of 1897) are centered on *contemplation of the Holy Face.* Since January 10, 1889 (date of her Clothing), Sister Thérèse of the Child Jesus added to her religious name the title "[and] of the Holy Face." She meditated quite often on the mysterious Suffering Servant of Deutero-Isaiah,[25] and this fascination for the "adorable Face of Jesus" never faded.

The canticle of August 12, 1895, attests to the permanence of this contemplation:

> Your Face is my only Homeland...
> Hiding myself in it unceasingly,
> I will resemble you, Jesus....[26]

Her brutal entry into the dark night, at Easter in 1896, rekindled her attraction for this "dear and veiled Face." From this follows, on August 6 of the same year (feast of the Transfiguration), her consecration to the Holy Face (Pri 12), the importance of which has perhaps not been emphasized enough by Theresian exegetes.

---

[23] Nevertheless, we must nuance this affirmation concerning Prayer 5. In this regard Thérèse writes to Céline: "I am trapped in the nets that do not appeal to me but are very useful to me in my present state of soul" (LT 144).

[24] This Prayer 20 was composed in July 1897. Forgetting her own terrible sufferings, she always keeps her concern for her novices.

[25] Cf. LT 87, 95, 98, 115. See also CJ 5.8.9 and DE, pp. 517–518.

[26] PN 20.3 and 5.

We have only to see the original text, painstakingly written in red and black ink, and the photographs of the three signatories who bear the title of the Holy Face,[27] to realize with what care Thérèse tried to solemnize it. Note also the strong apostolic inspiration ("we need souls ...") that, in this period, corresponds well to the expansion of her missionary desire.

This desire was sharply stimulated a few months earlier by an unforeseen event that touched her deeply. Mother Agnes of Jesus entrusted to her a seminarian, Abbé Bellière, so that she could help him spiritually.[28] Once again, one of her most cherished desires—to have a priest-brother—had just been fulfilled in an unexpected way. She quickly composed an apostolic prayer that is also, in its way, an act of offering because she "joyfully offers *all* the *prayers* and *sacrifices*" at her disposal (Pri 8) for this future missionary.

Moreover, when we realize how intensely she lived this gift of herself in 1895, we glimpse what powerful grace will surround the aspirant to the priesthood! On February 24, 1897, she will ask him to say "every day" this prayer for her: "Merciful Father, in the name of our Sweet Jesus, the Virgin Mary and all the Saints, I ask you to enkindle your Spirit of Love in my sister and to grant her the grace of making you greatly loved." [29]

The picture of the Holy Face that Thérèse made for her breviary (Pri 14 and 16), parallel to that of the Child Jesus (Pri 13 and 15), manifests the increased desire to resemble and to identify with the Christ Child and the suffering Christ. Although quite exhausted, she will pose before Céline's camera on June 7, 1897,[30] holding two pictures to leave a visual testament of her religious

---

[27] Thérèse, Céline (who was then called Geneviève of Saint Thérèse, Marie of the Holy Face) and Marie of the Trinity and of the Holy Face.

[28] Ms C, 32r.

[29] LT 220. She had asked P. Roulland for this same prayer (LT 189, LC 166, 171, 175, and LT 201). In LT 221 (March 19, 1897), she modifies the formula.

[30] VTL 41, 42, 43 (used as cover photo of present volume).

name, which sums up her vocation and her "mission." [31] "I am the
Jesus of Thérèse," says the Child Jesus with his finger pointing toward heaven. "I am the Jesus of Thérèse," murmurs the Holy Face
with his eyes lowered. "I am Thérèse of the Child Jesus and of the
Holy Face," echoes in reply the one who will soon enter into her
passion, following in Jesus' footsteps to Gethsemane.

The prayers inspired by Joan of Arc (Pri 17)—not yet canon-
ized—St. Sebastian, and the Holy Innocents (Pri 18), express the
Theresian struggle as it enters a critical phase at the end of 1896
and beginning of 1897; a combat of faith, combat against her illness, of which certain symptoms announced her approaching end.
By herself shedding "[her] heart's blood," she wants to encourage
her sister Céline who, as a novice, is also having a hard struggle in
following her Carmelite vocation (Pri 17).

In the infirmary, at the end of her strength, Thérèse writes
another pedagogical prayer for Sister Martha, who would be thirty-
two on the feast of Our Lady of Mount Carmel, "for acquiring humility" (Pri 20). This meditation on the "annihilations" of Jesus, on
Sister Martha's own weakness and the appeal to Mercy, is also about
the realities that the invalid is experiencing. Soon, at the height of
her agony, she will dare to assert boldly: "Yes, I have understood
humility of heart ... I think that I am humble...." [32]

Three weeks earlier she had written with difficulty her last
autograph, a prayer addressed to Mary, on the feast of Mary's Na-
tivity, the seventh anniversary of her profession.[33]

To mark out this journey, two spontaneous prayers stand out
like two mountains of unequal height dominating the plains and
hills: her Profession Note of September 8, 1890, and the Act of
Oblation of June 9, 1895.

The first, with its anguished writing, expresses "both a child's
consternation and a warrior's determination." [34] The name of

---

[31] LT 109.

[32] CJ 30.9; DE, 382 [HLC, p. 205].

[33] September 8, 1890, date of the composition of Pri 2.

[34] Père Marie-François de Ste. Marie, Mss II, p. 53.

Jesus—whom Thérèse addresses in the familiar "tu" [35]—appears eight times in twenty-three lines. "What a prayer! The seeds of all the others are contained in this note," remarks a commentator.[36]

The second dominates the whole collection. Here for the first time is a critical edition of the famous "Act of Oblation of [her-]self as Victim of Holocaust to the Merciful Love of God."

The historical circumstances of the Act of Oblation related in these pages, some of which are previously unpublished, confirm the opinion of those who, following Abbé André Combes, see in Thérèse's new orientation of spirituality "one of the most moving and momentous revolutions the Holy Spirit has unleashed in the spiritual evolution of humanity." [37]

We had to limit ourselves in order not to add to the many commentaries on the Act of Oblation and in order to give only the notes that are indispensable for an ever-more-accurate understanding of an important text, the consequence of her discovery of the way of childhood made several months earlier. Mother Agnes of Jesus wanted to submit it to the approbation of the church before allowing it to be proposed to the sisters (which Thérèse had spontaneously done for Céline and probably for Marie of the Sacred Heart). Père Armand Constant Lemonnier's only correction did not convince her, but she accepted it out of obedience.[38] Since then, millions of copies of the Act of Oblation in every language have spread throughout the world.

We must put each of these prayers back in its chronological place in the Theresian itinerary so as to grasp its full value. As in all her other writings, the Carmelite put a great deal of herself into

---

[35] "I like to say *Tu* also, because that more truly expresses the intimate love I have for [Jesus]. I always address Him this way in my conversations with Him, but I do not dare to do so in my poems and prayers when they are to be read by others" (CSG, p. 82; *Memoir,* p. 110).

[36] M. F. Lacan, *Sur une prière de la Petite Thérèse,* Bulletin of the Abbey of Hautecombe, no. 138, 1985, pp. 7–8.

[37] André Combes, *Introduction à la spiritualité de Sainte Thérèse de l'Enfant Jésus,* 2d ed. (Paris: Vrin, 1948), p. 184. Cf. Combes, *The Spirituality of St. Thérèse: An Introduction* (Dublin: M. H. Gill & Son, 1950), p. 52.

[38] CG, p. 809+d. Cf. pp. 62–63 below.

these various texts whose sometimes conventional language must not hide how radically appropriate they were to her life. She knew all too well the traps that threaten the authors of "beautiful prayers," easy to write, hard to live. Not for a moment does she want to add anthology texts to the countless books of piety that line— and sometimes clutter—community libraries. Her prayers sprang from needs: an interior need for the eleven spontaneous texts, a sisterly need to help her sisters, a seminarian, a married woman. Each time Thérèse expresses herself with clarity and truthfulness.

Here, then, is the final treasure she leaves us, this young warrior who wrote in her last manuscript: "It is prayer, it is sacrifice that give me all my strength; these are the invincible weapons that Jesus has given me. They can touch souls much better than words, as I have very frequently experienced." [39]

A Life of Prayer

"Sister Thérèse thought of God unceasingly. I asked her one day: 'How do you think of God always?' She answered: 'It isn't difficult; we naturally think of the one we love.' 'Then,' I said, 'you never lose his presence?' 'Oh, no,' she said, 'I do not believe I have ever been three minutes at a time without thinking of Him.' " [40]

Sister Marie of the Sacred Heart's testimony at the process of beatification and canonization of Thérèse sums up very well the prayer life of her young sister. "Her life was a continual prayer," she will say again. [41]

From earliest childhood to her last illness, Thérèse's life could be framed by two sayings that illustrate the evolution of her prayer— a prayer that became continual, the horizon hoped for by all whom the Spirit draws onto the path of the search for God.

Having reached the age of four, Thérèse could well see herself "a cloistered religious" with Céline. But as Pauline explains to her that she will have to keep silence, the child, perplexed, wonders

---

[39] Ms C, 24v.

[40] Sister Marie of the Sacred Heart, PA 231; cf. PO 246; CSG, p. 77.

[41] PA, 236.

how "to pray to Jesus without saying anything?" [42] Twenty years later, ill and without any human hope of being cured, Sister Thérèse converses with Céline (who had become Sister Geneviève):

"I cannot sleep, I am suffering too much, so I pray..."

"And what do you say to Jesus?"

"I don't say anything, I love him." [43]

The life inscribed between these two remarks—childhood at Alençon and Lisieux, nine years in Carmel—is rooted in prayer under all its forms: memorized or spontaneous prayer, mental prayer, Mass, Divine Office, prayers written on holy cards or elsewhere. Carmelite life obviously favored to the highest degree this intimate call to union with God, as the central precept of the Rule requires that "each one remain in his cell or nearby it, meditating day and night on the law of the Lord and watching in prayer unless occupied with other necessary work." [44]

We must also not forget that after the great sensible joys she felt as an adolescent, [45] Sister Thérèse experienced very quickly in Carmel the rigors of the most devastating dryness. [46] This was before entering, at Easter of 1896, her most terrible trial of faith, which

---

[42] CG I, p. 97, letter of Pauline Martin, April 4, 1877 [GC I, p. 108].

[43] DE, p. 610. Cf. "And I can't pray! I can only look at the Blessed Virgin and say 'Jesus' " (Geneviève in DE 16.8; DE, p. 605 [HLC, p. 228]).

[44] Text read every Friday in the refectory during Thérèse's time, cf. BT, p. 11, note 7.

[45] Ms A, 52r.

[46] Many confessions in Ms A, 73v; 75v; 76r; Ms B, 1r; Ms C, 25v, cf. LT 57, 74, 75, 78, 110, 111, 112, etc. Let us not forget Sister Marie of the Trinity's testimony, related by P. Philippe of the Trinity: "Sister Thérèse of the Child Jesus would have slept during prayer if she had not 'dipped' into her book of the Gospels. In summer there were six hours of sleep during the night, plus the siesta. She bent over, she fell forward during Mass. She slept almost without stopping during her thanksgiving, on her knees with her head to the floor. She could not resist.... She was sleeping and she spent her time running after her sleep." (*Thérèse de Lisieux. La Sainte de l'Enfance spirituelle* [Thérèse of Lisieux. Saint of Spiritual Childhood], Lethielleux 1980, p. 25). Let us recall that during Mass and prayer, Carmelites sat back on their heels.

would last until the day of her death eighteen months later. Then it seemed to her that "everything had disappeared" and that she was going toward "the night of nothingness." [47] "It is true that at times a very small ray of the sun comes to illumine my darkness and then the trial ceases for *an instant,* but afterward the memory of this ray, instead of causing me joy, makes my darkness even more dense." [48]

From her earliest childhood in Alençon, Thérèse Martin basked in the atmosphere of family prayer: morning and evening prayers, grace at meals, their life moving to the tempo of the important moments of the liturgical cycle, the feasts of the saints, the month of Mary.[49]

According to her mother, the first time "little Thérèse" prayed goes back to when she was two-and-a half. "She said out loud to me in Church: 'I was at Mass. I really prayed to God!' [49a] When her father returned in the evening and she did not see him on his knees she said to him: 'Why, Papa, are you not saying your prayers?' " [50]

If they put her to bed without her having said her devotions, there was the same agitation: "When I went to bed, she told me she had not said her prayers. I answered, 'Sleep, you will say them tomorrow.' But she did not give up her idea. To end it, her father made her say them with him, but he did not know how to say all she was accustomed to reciting and, then, he had 'to ask the grace of…' He did not understand what she meant by this. Finally he said something quite close to it in order to satisfy her, and we had peace until the next morning." [51]

---

[47] Ms C, 6v.

[48] Ms C, 7v.

[49] Cf. Zélie Martin, *Correspondance Familiale,* and Stéphane-Joseph Piat, *The Story of a Family: The Home of the Little Flower* (New York: P. J. Kenedy & Sons, 1947), pp. 150ff. Cf. Mother Agnes in PO, 153.

[49a] [Thérèse says *mette* for *messe* (Mass) and *pridez* for *prié* (prayed).–Trans.]

[50] CG II, p. 1115 (March 14, 1875).

[51] Version of Sr. Marie of the Trinity in *Correspondance Familiale,* VT 93 (January 1984): 73. Cf. CG II, p. 1118 [GC II, p. 1218].

In this regard, we could sum up her childhood at Alençon with an excerpt from a letter of Mme. Martin that Thérèse copied in her first manuscript: "The little one is our whole happiness. She will be good; one can already see the germ of goodness in her. She speaks only about God and wouldn't miss her prayers for anything."[52]

The mother's role shows up better when she is not there. Exiled to Mme. Leriche's home during the last phase of Zélie Martin's illness, Céline and Thérèse were disturbed. They did not say their prayers that morning. "Well, my little girls, you will say them," said the aunt and she left the two forlorn sisters alone in a room. "Oh! this is not like Mama! She always had us say our prayers with her."[53]

After their mother's death, the family fervently kept up the Alençon rituals at Les Buissonnets. Pauline took over from their mother. "In the morning you used to come to me and ask me if I had raised my heart to God, and then you dressed me. While dressing me you spoke about Him and afterward we knelt down and said our prayers together."[54] In the evening, at the family gathering, she turned to her father "to see how the saints pray."[55] Every day on their afternoon walks they visited a church together. Near a stream where her father was fishing, Thérèse went apart. "Without knowing what it was to meditate, my soul was absorbed in real prayer."[56] But she noticed that it was in her bed where she made her "profound meditations."[57]

During her school years with the Benedictines of the Abbey, she kept this custom of praying, although lamenting that no one taught her a method. Hence her detailed questioning of

---

[52] Ms A, 11r; cf. CG II, p. 1130 [GC II, p. 1223].

[53] Ms A, 12r.

[54] Ms A, 13v.

[55] Ms A, 18r.

[56] Ms A, 14v.

[57] Ms A, 31r.

Marguerite[58] and her sister Henriette[59] on how to set about doing it. Later, she wrote: "I understand now that I was making mental prayer without knowing it and that God was already instructing me in secret."[60] He will remain her only spiritual director.

At the time of her First Communion, she made the resolution to recite each day a Memorare to the Blessed Virgin (cf. VT, no 74, p. 134).

After her "conversion" of Christmas 1886, the adolescent received a flood of graces. She recalled her conversations in the belvedere at Les Buissonnets with her sister Céline: "It appears we were receiving graces like those granted to the great saints...."[61] "I was growing in love for God; I felt within my heart certain aspirations unknown until then, and at times I had veritable transports of love."[62]

Her entrance into Carmel on April 9, 1888, definitively immersed her in a life organized to give priority to prayer in all its forms: personal prayer marking the day from rising to sleeping, with two hours of silent prayer in choir; communal prayer, including about three hours and a half of choral office and one hour for Mass. The goal, with the help of divine grace, was to attain as fully as possible to continual prayer, a state of union with God, whether perceived or not. Let us note that vocal prayers held a considerable place in this religious universe of the end of the nineteenth century.[63]

Sister Thérèse affirmed to Mother Marie de Gonzague that she did not at all hold in contempt these numerous communal

---

[58] She became Sister Marie of the Holy Rosary, O.S.B., PO 554. Cf. *La petite Thérèse à l'Abbaye*, Notre-Dame du Pré, 1930, pp. 23–24.

[59] Ms A, 33v and *La petite Thérèse à l'Abbaye*, pp. 42–43. Another witness: Sister Saint Francis de Sales, O.S.B., PO, 548.

[60] Ms A, 33v.

[61] Ms A, 48r.

[62] Ms A, 52r.

[63] The goal of continual prayer remains the same today, but the renewal of religious life that followed the Council of Vatican II reduced the number of vocal prayers in Carmel.

prayers: "However, I would not want you to believe, dear Mother, that I recite without devotion the prayers said in common in the choir. [...] On the contrary, I love very much these prayers in common, for Jesus has promised *to be in the midst of those who gather together in His name.* I feel then that the fervor of my Sisters makes up for my lack of fervor; but when alone (I am ashamed to admit it) the recitation of the rosary is more difficult for me than the wearing of an instrument of penance. I feel I say it so poorly! I force myself in vain to meditate on the mysteries of the rosary; I don't succeed in fixing my mind on them." [64]

The Prayer of a Life

As a being of praise, Thérèse has but one goal: "to sing the Mercies of the Lord." [65] This is the central theme of her Autobiographical Manuscripts: to give thanks for the gratuitous love she has received. Elizabeth of the Trinity, her spiritual sister in the Carmel of Dijon, will want to be "a praise of glory." [66] Thérèse is one also. Her voice was not very beautiful, nor was she a musician like Elizabeth Catez, yet she did not hesitate to compare her life to a song: "I shall sing even when I must gather my flowers in the midst of thorns.... These songs of love from the littlest of hearts will charm *You.*" [67] Let us not forget that all her poems were in fact sung canticles.

As for the prayer of petition, she practices it habitually and does not doubt she is heard. Having many times experienced that her desires were heard beyond her hopes, for the Lord himself

---

[64] Ms C, 25 v. Cf. "When I think of how much trouble I've had all my life trying to recite the rosary!" (CJ 20.8.16 [HLC, p. 160]).

[65] Ms A, 2r; 3v; 4r; 40r; 86r; Ms C, 1r; 3r; 27v; 29v; 34r.

[66] Eph 1:14.

[67] Ms B, 4v. Cf. "...Repeating your praise, that is my only delight" (PN 34, R. 3); "You teach me to sing divine praises" (PN 54.7.3). Cf. The explanation of her coat of arms: "The harp again represents Thérèse who wanted to sing eternally melodies of love to Jesus" (Ms A, 85v).

placed them in her heart,[68] she does not fear to express her requests with the boldness of a child: "I desire," [69] "I hope," [70] "I want." [71]

Her hope is founded on Jesus' words, "all that you ask the Father in my name, He will grant," quoting John 16:23.[72] With the whole church, she makes all her prayers, and first and foremost her Act of Offering, pass through Christ, the one Mediator. The granting of it she leaves to God. A refrain runs through her writings: "My prayer was answered to the letter." [73] "I felt in the bottom of my heart that my prayer was answered." [74] "Jesus deigned to answer me," [75] and so on.

Recalling the prayer of intercession she made with her novice, Marie of the Trinity, for the conversion of the latter's sister, Thérèse remarks: "Oh! infinite mercy of the Lord, who really wants to answer the prayer of His little children.... How great is the power of *Prayer!* One could call it a Queen who has at each instant free access to the King and who is able to obtain whatever she asks." [76]

Thérèse also becomes this queen interceding with the King,[77] especially on the day of her profession: "What graces I begged for on that day! I really felt I was the Queen and so I profited from my

---

[68] She found this axiom in Saint John of the Cross (cf. letter 15 to Sister Leonor, in K-RJ), the pillar on which her invincible hope rests: Ms A, 71r; 84v; Ms C, 31r; LT 201 and 253; CJ 13.7.15; CSG, p. 51 (*Memoir,* p. 58).

[69] Ms A, 43r; 52r; 54v; 82v.

[70] Ms A, 15r; 32r; 53v; 64v; 67r; Ms B, 2v; 5v; Ms C, 8v; 33v.

[71] Ms A, 76v; Ms B, 2v; cf. 3r (sixteen times); 5r–v; Ms C, 12v; 25r; 33v.

[72] Ms C, 35v.

[73] Ms A, 46r.

[74] Ms A, 61r.

[75] Ms A, 82r.

[76] Ms C, 25r.

[77] Ms A, 35r; Ms B, 4r. Cf. "I can obtain everything when mysteriously I speak heart to heart with my Divine King" (PN 32.2).

title by delivering captives, by obtaining favors from the *King* for His ungrateful subjects, finally, I wanted to deliver all the souls from purgatory and convert all sinners. I prayed very much for my *Mother,* my dear Sisters, my whole family, but especially for my poor Father, who was so tried and so *saintly.*" [78] A new Esther, but even more a new Joan of Arc, this young warrior trusts in "her invincible weapons," "prayer and sacrifice." [79]

This prayer of intercession, essential to her vocation as Carmelite,[80] will become more and more important as she approaches her end. For a long time she was still able to intercede for sinners by name (Pranzini, ex-Father Hyacinthe Loyson, Diana Vaughan-Léo Taxil)[81] but as her mission expands—thanks, among other things, to her responsibility toward two missionary brothers—her prayer encircles the whole world. On her death bed, she can no longer detail "for the Church, for France... for Peter... for Paul..." [82] because she is suffering too much, but also because she is interceding for the universe, anticipating the universal intercession of her life after death. But in Thérèse we never find anything systematic; she continues to pray particularly for M. Tostain[83] and offers her last communion for Hyacinthe Loyson.[84]

Never has she better expressed her identification with Christ than when she boldly appropriates, with a remarkable theological correctness, Jesus' own prayer testament (Jn 17). Sister Thérèse will leave this world and enter "into Life." [85] She rereads Christ's farewell to his disciples on Holy Thursday, copies the gospel passage

---

[78] Ms A, 76v.

[79] Ms C, 24v; 32r; LT 226; RP 8, 4v, 40. Cf. *Mes Armes,* p. 121.

[80] "I came to save souls and especially to pray for priests" (Ms A, 69v).

[81] Cf. "I prayed very much for Monsieur de Virville" (LT 42); "I will continue to pray unceasingly for good Monsieur David" (LT 59), and so on.

[82] CJ 4.8.8. [HLC, p. 133].

[83] CJ 2.9.7. [HLC, p. 181].

[84] CJ 19.8. [HLC, p. 157]. Cf. DE, 173.

[85] LT 244.

while adapting it to herself and putting it in the feminine: "Perhaps this is boldness? No, for a long time You permitted me to be bold with You. You have said to me as the father of the prodigal son said to his older son: *'EVERYTHING that is mine is yours.'* Your words, O Jesus, are mine, then, and I can make use of them to draw upon the souls united to me the favors of the heavenly Father." [86]

Offered as a victim of holocaust wholly consumed[87] who espouses Christ's own oblative prayer, meditating day and night on the Word, she has become in her turn a "Word of God" [88] for the world.

Exhausted by her sufferings, she leaves her last Autobiographical Manuscript unfinished. While she is making her thanksgiving after Holy Communion, she has a flash of inspiration. This light springs from a verse of the Song of Songs: "Draw me, we shall run in the odor of your ointments" (1.3). Thérèse continues: "O Jesus, it is not even necessary to say: *"When drawing me, draw the souls whom I love!"* This simple statement: *"Draw me"* suffices. I understand, Lord, that when a soul allows herself to be captivated by *the odor of your ointments,* she cannot run alone, all the souls whom she loves follow in her train." [89]

Hans Urs von Balthasar comments:

> The little Thérèse is the first to rid contemplation of its Neoplatonic relics; this fact alone is sufficient to guarantee her place in the history of theology. In fact, though not in so many words, she has substituted the notion of fruitfulness for that of effectiveness. She is the first to see quite clearly that action is not simply an effect of overflowing contemplation...but that contemplation in

---

[86] Ms C, 34v.

[87] She gives herself to God "to be no more" (PN 51.3.6).

[88] Pius XI, discourse in Italian, February 11, 1923, at the time of the promulgation of the Decree concerning the approbation of the miracles for the beatification of Thérèse.

[89] Ms C, 34r.

itself is a dynamic force and is indeed the source of all fruitfulness, the first [lever][90] in all change.

...Thérèse acquires an attitude that cannot be described exactly in terms of either contemplation or action; she is beyond them both in the all-embracing law of love, which governs both receptivity and fruitfulness, both Mary and Martha.[91] This transcendent point of unity is the ultimate knowledge granted to Thérèse.

...Here Thérèse touches upon the second formula governing action and contemplation, not Thomas' formula but that of Ignatius. Except that it is better reversed in the case of the Carmelite Thérèse: *in contemplatione activus.* [92]

"Into the Flames of His Love ..." [93]

Let us imagine the worst and suppose for a few moments that all we had were these twenty-one prayers of Thérèse and that her other writings had disappeared. What image would they give us of this young Carmelite? [94]

First of all they reveal in the one who composed them an impassioned love of God whom she sometimes calls "adorable and blessed Trinity," "Lord," "Father," and sometimes and above all "Jesus." For Thérèse he is "the Son," her "Spouse," and her "King." What fascinates her is the "Love" that he showed her by his "annihilations," of which the Crib, the Cross, and the Eucharist are the stages of a more and more incredible self-abasement. What a thirst for "Love" in this gentle and humble "Sacred Heart!"

---

[90] Image employed by Thérèse in reference to Archimedes (Ms C, 36r).

[91] Ms C, 36r.

[92] Hans Urs von Balthasar. *Two Sisters in the Spirit: Thérèse of Lisieux and Elizabeth of the Trinity* (San Francisco: Ignatius Press, 1992) pp. 195, 198, 197.

[93] Ms C, 36r.

[94] In the following paragraphs the quoted words and phrases are from the prayers themselves.

Plunged into this "furnace" of his merciful Love, the Carmelite can only "love Him and make Him loved" and offer herself to him as a "Victim of holocaust" to be wholly consumed by this fire of Trinitarian Love.

This Act of Oblation bathes all the prayers with the light of its fire, but the gift of "every beat of her heart," of her actions, is often present in many other texts. This attitude has become habitual with Thérèse, who is wholly given to her "Beloved," whose only desire is to be in an "eternal Face to Face" so she might receive his "kiss."

While waiting, this "adorable Face" appears to her with a beauty that enraptures her soul and she unceasingly contemplates it so that his "likeness" may be imprinted in her. Since God "has hidden," she in turn wants to hide herself "in the secret of his Face."

In this life, how is she "to console" Jesus for the ingratitude of "poor sinners," for the lukewarmness of priests and religious, for sins and for "blasphemies," unless by "prayer and sacrifice" so as to "save many souls." With all her strength Thérèse aspires to the ultimate witness, "martyrdom," the "gift of her blood."

While hoping for this unsurpassable grace, each day we must do "God's will": Thérèse repeats this to her novices and to a layperson. Here we have the daily combat of this young warrior, emulator of "Saint Sebastian" and of "Joan of Arc," who wants "to fight for the Love of Jesus until the evening of her life." She knows her "weaknesses," her "failings," her "miseries," but "she does not become discouraged." In the midst of her trial of faith, she wants to remain a child and does not give up "aspiring to be a saint," for God Himself "will be her Sanctity." If she has suffered much during her life, yet she does not rely on any of her merits: she will appear before Jesus with "empty hands."

From all her prayers there breathes forth a bold faith, "the confidence" of a child who relies on the very word of God. We see here her familiarity with Sacred Scripture; in her prayers there are more than fifty biblical quotations, nor does she forget her Father St. John of the Cross. Prayer 12 has as its heading the famous passage:

> For a little of this pure Love is more beneficial to the
> Church...than all these other works put together.... It is

of the greatest importance that we make many acts of Love so that being consumed quickly we do not linger long here on earth but soon attain to the vision of Jesus, Face to Face.

"To love, to make Him loved," the apostolic mission of the Carmelite is expressed persistently. The thirst of Christ devours her: "Souls, Lord, we need souls." She shares fully the Trinitarian Love for the countless created beings and unceasingly surrenders her life so that they may experience this love.

If we conclude this brief synthesis by noting that this daughter of Saint Teresa of Avila greatly loves the Virgin Mary, "her Mother," "Queen of Carmel" and of "Heaven" to whom she entrusts her offering and to whom she addresses the first and last prayers in this collection, we will agree that this volume alone sketches a spiritual portrait of the Saint of Lisieux quite close to the very precise picture revealed by the ensemble of her writings.

Why should we be surprised at this? Sister Thérèse prayed as she lived: "For simple souls there must be no complicated ways," she wrote.[95] In her prayers we find her, whole and entire, at the different stages of her life: religious profession (September 8, 1895), Offering to Merciful Love (June 9, 1895), "mistress of novices," sister to two missionaries (1895–1896), fighting until the end in her trial of faith and hope (Easter 1896), consecrating herself to the Holy Face (August 6, 1896), dying of love in humility (summer 1897).

Resituated in the "truth of *life*," [96] these twenty-one prayers merit then to enter into "The Prayer Treasury of All Time," [97] not as petrified texts, but as the still imperfect expression of this radiating flame that Thérèse has become: "You put This Fire from Heaven in my soul." [98] The outcome of this life of prayer is the offering of herself as a victim of holocaust, which she will explain

---

[95] Ms C, 33v.

[96] Ms A, 31v.

[97] Cf. the anthology published under this title by Sister Geneviève, O.P., *Foi Vivante*, no. 173, Cerf, 1981. Thérèse is quoted there on pp. 124–127.

[98] PN 24.17.3. Cf. CSG, 71 (*Memoir*, pp. 77-78).

during her last conversations in the infirmary, until the agony of September 30, 1897: "I do not regret having surrendered myself to Love. Oh no! I don't regret it; just the opposite! [...] My God ... I love you!" [99]

Henceforth, throughout the whole world, countless people would be inspired and warmed at this inextinguishable flame.

Had not Sister Thérèse written at the end of her last Autobiographical Manuscript:

> This is my prayer. I ask Jesus to draw me into the flames of His love, to unite me so closely to Him that He [may] live and act in me. I feel that the more the fire of love burns within my heart, the more I shall say: *"Draw me,"* the more also the souls who will approach me (poor little piece of iron, useless if I withdraw from the divine furnace), the more these souls *will run swiftly in the odor of the ointments of their Beloved,* for a soul that is burning with love cannot remain inactive.[100]

Guy Gaucher, O.C.D.

---

[99] CJ 30.9 [HLC, p. 205].

[100] Ms C, 36r.

The Prayers

Pri 1: Thérèse first prayer, to Mary
*O my good Blessed Virgin, grant that your little Thérèse
may stop tormenting herself.*

Pri 21: Thérèse last prayer, to Mary
*O Mary, if I were Queen of Heaven and you were Thérèse, I would want
to be Thérèse so that you might be Queen of Heaven!!!..............*

Prayer 1

"O My Good Blessed Virgin"

O my good Blessed Virgin, grant that your little Thérèse may stop tormenting herself.

DOCUMENT: autograph. afs 20.8 x 13.1 cm. Two lines in ink, in Thérèse's writing, followed by a poem copied by Sister Agnes of Jesus.

DATE: June (?) 1884. A study of the content shows that the compliment in verse (24 octosyllables) was composed by Sister Agnes "For Mother Marie de Gonzague" for her feast on June 21. It is after Thérèse's first communion (May 8, 1884), to which she alludes. Thus, Thérèse probably wrote her prayer around June 21. The handwriting is that of 1884.

CIRCUMSTANCES: What was "tormenting" the child Thérèse to justify this cry to Mary? The *Story of a Soul* seems to supply the answer: "...but the Blessed Virgin permitted this torment for my soul's good" (Ms A, 31r). Let us recall the facts: On May 13, 1883, Thérèse was cured of a nervous illness by the Blessed Virgin's smile. At first she wanted to keep her secret but her older sister Marie found out and told the Carmelites, etc. The child began to doubt and believed she "lied." They had robbed her of her "happiness." After that she felt only "humiliation" and "profound horror" (ibid.). Her suffering had been going on for a year when Thérèse begged the Blessed Virgin to free her from it. She experienced a period of calm "for nearly a whole year" but definitive liberation did not take place until November 4, 1887, at Our Lady of Victories in Paris, when "the Blessed Virgin made me feel it was really she who had smiled on me" (Ms A, 56v). To emphasize the acuteness of the child Thérèse's suffering, let us note that in her autobiography the word "torment" does not appear again until she uses it in connection with her trial of faith (Ms C, 5v, 6v). There, a great happiness—"the thought of Heaven"—has just been snatched from Thérèse. Thus, we can rightly compare this little Pri 1 to the cry of distress of Pri 19.

O my good Blessed Virgin: an appeal Thérèse utters again on her deathbed (CJ 30.9.6 [HLC, p. 204]); cf. also LT 137 and CJ 28.8.9).

Prayer 2

[Profession Note]

September 8, 1890

O Jesus, my divine spouse! May I never lose the second robe of my Baptism! Take me before I can commit the slightest voluntary fault. May I never seek nor find anything but yourself alone. May creatures be nothing [5]for me and may I be nothing for them, but may you, Jesus, be *everything!*... May the things of earth never be able to trouble my soul, and may nothing disturb my peace. Jesus, I ask you for nothing but peace, and also love, infinite love without any limits other than yourself; love that is no [10]longer I but you, my Jesus. Jesus, may I die a martyr for you. Give me martyrdom of heart or of body, or rather give me both..... Give me the grace to fulfill my vows in all their perfection, and make me understand what a real spouse of yours should be. Never let me be [15]a burden to the community, let nobody be occupied with me, let me be looked on as one to be trampled underfoot, forgotten like your little grain of sand, Jesus.

May your will be done in me perfectly, and may I arrive at the place you have prepared for me......

[20]Jesus, allow me to save very many souls; let no soul be lost today; let all the souls in purgatory be saved....Jesus, pardon me if I say anything I should not say. I want only to give you joy and to console you.

DOCUMENT: afs 10 x 13.3 cm, irregular shape, yellowed paper, faded ink.
Several revisions: some by Thérèse as she wrote it, others by Mother

Agnes of Jesus (different ink and handwriting). On the back: "Note that Sr. Thérèse wore over her heart on her Profession Day" (Mother Agnes).

DATE: Probably September 7, eve of her profession, although Thérèse dates it the day itself, "September 8, 1890."

COPY: CE I, 88v–89r, which inserts it in Manuscript A, at the time of the account of her profession (76v–77r) between "to place any obstacle in the way" and "This beautiful day." The copyist, Sr. Madeleine of Jesus, introduces it thus: "On that day, the Servant of God wore over her heart the following little note we found fastened to her vows after her death, and which we inserted in the manuscript."

PUBLICATION: HA 98, pp. 127f., where the prayer is put in the second person plural and partly rewritten. The facsimile of the format is inset in the photocopy edition of Ms A between folios 76 and 77. An enlarged reproduction is given in the "Appended Pieces" of the same edition (1956).

CIRCUMSTANCES: On Thérèse's dispositions at the time of her profession cf. Ms A, 75r–77v and the letters written during her ten-day preparatory retreat (CG I, pp. 551–553; GCI, pp. 643–673). In writing this note, Thérèse makes her own a traditional custom. At that time it was usual for the novice on her Clothing Day [reception of the habit] or the professed nun on the day of her vows to wear over her heart a note in which she asked for herself and for her friends the graces she desired to obtain. A tradition held that every prayer made at the time of the great prostration—arms in the form of a cross, on a rough carpet—is answered; cf. for example: *Meditations for a Clothing Retreat in Carmel* (Tours: Mame, 1873), p. 128, or *Spiritual Direction... for Novices* (Poitiers: Oudin, 1869), pp. 194f.

NOTES
(The number refers to the line of the autograph):

1–2: *the second robe of my baptism:* a long spiritual tradition sees in religious profession a "second baptism" that gives back to the soul her "robe of innocence" (Pri 5, 8r). That such a request should open Thérèse's prayer reveals her anxiety at that time on the subject of sin; cf. LT 114 and Ms A, 70r. Later, the discovery of her "little way" opens her to quite other perspectives; cf. Ms A, 84r; LT 182 ("innocence *superior* to that of Baptism").

3: *the slightest voluntary fault:* cf. LT 114. Thérèse will never commit a deliberate sin, but will place herself with an ever-increasing peace in the hands of Divine Mercy.

4–6: *creatures...nothing...Jesus...everything:* doubtless echoes the *Imitation of Christ*, but also St. John of the Cross in whose writings Thérèse immersed herself for the whole of 1890 (cf. Ms A, 83r).

9–10: *love that is no longer I but You:* beneath a very simple vocabulary, Thérèse in fact asks for "transformation of love" through which the Beloved and the soul "exchange self for the other" (St. John of the Cross, *Spiritual Canticle*, for example, st. 12, 7).

11: *martyrdom:* one of Thérèse's deep desires since she was a child; cf. Ms B, 3r; Mss III, p. 124; CG II, p. 1373; *Poésies*, vol. 2, p. 337; RP, p. 430. In 1896 she will affirm that her "desires for martyrdom are nothing" (LT 197). But she will experience "martyrdom of the body" through illness; cf. DE, passim; and many kinds of "martyrdom of the heart" (cf. LT 167 and 213).

17: *grain of sand:* one of Thérèse's favorite symbols since March, 1888; cf. LT 45 and LT 114. But after her profession it will not reappear until June 1897 (Ms C, 2v). We know that she borrows the image from General de Sonis (cf. CG II, p. 1170 and VT, January 1980, p. 73).

19: *the place You have prepared for me:* cf. Jn 14:2–3.

20–22: *allow me...to save:* cf Ms A, 76v, which transposes this as "convert sinners." Already at her Clothing, Thérèse expresses the same desire (LT 74). In her canonical examination, September 2, 1890, she insists on the apostolic orientation of her vocation: "to save souls" (Ms A, 69v).

22: *souls in purgatory...saved:* as in LT 74. But the Act of Oblation will speak of "liberating" them (Pri 6. 7–8). Even in the infirmary Thérèse will keep her concern for "souls in purgatory"; cf. LT 182, 3; CJ 18.5.2, 6.8.4, 11.9.5 [HLC, pp. 45, 137, 188], etc. At an unknown date, she had made "the heroic act" (or abandonment of her merits) for them (cf. PA, 178 and 286f.).

23: *give you joy:* to give Jesus joy, give him pleasure, to make him happy, such was the ultimate purpose of Thérèse's whole existence (Ms A, 2v; C, 7r and 28v; LT 211, 246, 261; PN 41 and 45.6; Pri 5.4).

24: *to console You:* cf. Pri 4 (two times); Pri 6 (two times), 9, and 12v. "To console Jesus" recurs often in Thérèse's letters (CG II, p. 1360), poems (vol. 2, p. 136), and plays (RP 2.3f., RP 3, 5, 7).

Prayer 3

A Look of Love at Jesus

Jesus, your little brides resolve to keep their eyes lowered in the refectory so that they may honor You and imitate the example You gave them when You were in Herod's presence. When that impious ruler mocked You, O Infinite Beauty, not a [5]complaint fell from your divine lips. You did not even deign to rest your adorable eyes on him. Oh! divine Jesus, doubtless Herod did not deserve a look from You, but we, your brides, want to attract your divine gaze toward us. We ask You to reward us with [10]a *look* of love every time we deprive ourselves of raising our eyes and we ask You not to refuse us this gentle *look* even when we fall, since we will count our failings. We will form a bouquet that you will not reject; we are confident of it. In these flowers You will see our desire to [15]love You and to resemble You, and You will bless your little children.

O Jesus! *look* on us with love and give us [181v] your sweet kiss.

Amen.

DOCUMENT; CE II, 181r–v, established in 1910 from the original. This must have disappeared after Sr. Martha's death (1916), as did most of her papers; cf. CG, p. 69. Same remark for Pri 4, 7, and 20.

DATE: 1893, according to CE II. In the absence of the autograph (the handwriting of which would have made possible a precise dating) we can keep this date as likely, even proposing July 1893; cf. note for line 12.

COMPOSED FOR: Sr. Martha of Jesus and herself. Professed since September 1890, they continued their novitiate under the direction of Mother Marie de Gonzague (appointed by Mother Agnes of Jesus, prioress, on February 20, 1893).

PUBLICATION: HA 14, p. 267 (revised text); HA 53, p. 256.

CIRCUMSTANCE: To preserve the spirit of solitude, even during meals in common, Carmelites are advised "always to keep their eyes lowered and directed in front of them, without turning their heads or looking at the others" (*Papier d'Exaction*, 1889, p. 23). It is not only out of fidelity "even to the point of scruple to all the written rules and customs" (CRM, pp. 72f.) that Thérèse abides by this ascetic practice. She lives in the presence of a Person, Jesus. It is for love of him that she lets "not one look" escape her (cf. Ms B, 4r). To lower her eyes is for her to "honor and imitate" the Man with the lowered eyes and closed lips, Jesus in His Passion, to liken herself to the Holy Face. This explains her strictness on this point not only with regard to Sr. Martha (cf. VT no. 101, p. 50) but also to Sr. Marie-Madeleine (CG II, p. 712, correcting the error of attribution), Marie of the Trinity (HA 53, p. 256 and LT 167), and above all, Sr. Marie of the Eucharist (VT no. 99, p. 11). To her she suggests a coredemptive dimension: "to save souls."

NOTES

Title: there is every reason to think it is by Thérèse herself; cf. PA, 590. The "look of love" theme is eminently Theresian and probably borrowed from John of the Cross. This mutual glance between Jesus (4 times) and the "bride" soul (2 times) is for her the symbol of the contemplative life.

3–4: *in Herod's presence:* cf. Lk: 23:9–11. Luke speaks only of Jesus'silence, but for Thérèse, Christ in his Passion is identified with the Holy Face, "lowered eyes" (LT 110, LT 87: CJ 5.8.7 [HLC p. 134]).

11–12: *and even when we fall:* this is the stroke of genius in such an apparently modest prayer, and is already the secret of Theresian reversal that gives dynamism to her "little way": to have enough bold "confidence" to offer her failings to Jesus as so many "flowers" (14). Let us emphasize that at the same period, "Jesus teaches her" (through St. John of the Cross) to "draw profit from everything, from the good and the bad she finds in herself" (LT 142, July 6, 1893, where she first quotes from the *Gloss on the Divine*). This bold attitude will become stronger still in Thérèse: not "to go hide herself in a corner to cry over her misery" (Ms B, 5r) but to run to Jesus to let herself "be punished with a kiss" (LT 258); to dare to tell him: "Let me offer it up to you just the same" (CJ 3.7.2).

12: *since we will count:* by inclination, Thérèse is loathe "to count" (LT 107; PN 17.5; LT 142). It is "out of charity" to Sr. Martha that she takes up her "chaplet of practices" again in July 1893 (LT 144); motive confirmed by Sr. Martha (PA, 414 and VT no. 101, pp. 49f.) and Sr. Geneviève (CSG, pp. 141f.). Thérèse agrees that at this period this asceticism is "very useful" to her (cf. LT 144).

Prayer 4

Homage to the Most Blessed Trinity

O my God, behold us as we bow before You. We come to beseech You for the grace of working for Your glory.

The blasphemies of sinners have sounded painfully in our ears. We wish to console You and to repair for the insults that souls redeemed by you make you [5]suffer. O adorable Trinity! we want to form a *concert* of all the little sacrifices we will make for Your love. For fifteen days, we will offer You the song of the little birds of Heaven who unceasingly praise you and reproach men and women for their ingratitude. [10]We will offer you also, O my God! the melody of musical instruments and we hope that our souls may merit to be a melodious lyre You can play to console Yourself for the indifference of so many souls who do not think of You. Likewise, for eight days we want to collect *diamonds* and [15]precious stones to repair for the eagerness of poor mortals [181r] who pursue passing riches without dreaming of those of eternity. O my God! grant us the grace to be more vigilant in seeking sacrifices than those who do not love you are in their pursuit of worldly goods.

[20]Finally, for eight days your children will gather the *fragrance* of flowers. By doing this they wish to make amends for all that priestly and religious souls make you suffer by their offenses. O blessed Trinity, grant us to be faithful and give us the grace to possess you after the exile of this life...

[25]Amen

DOCUMENT: CE II, 180v–181r, text established in 1910 according to the original, which has since disappeared; cf. p. 60. But two sheets (13.2 x 10.6 cm), not filed at the Process, were found. These detail for each day the images evoked in the prayer: birds, musical instruments, etc.

DATE: February 1894, judging by the paper and handwriting of the two sheets. Thus, we must exclude the date "1892" proposed by CE II and HA 53, p. 255. According to the sheets, the counting of sacrifices lasts five weeks, which corresponded to Lent 1894 (Ash Wednesday: February 7). The effort could have been sustained either from February 11 to March 18 or February 18 to Easter (March 25). At the same time, Sr. Marie-Madeleine received a sheet of "Practices for Lent" but in a different style, also valid for five weeks; cf. CG II, p. 712.

COMPOSED FOR: herself and Sr. Martha. At her own request, Thérèse remained in the novitiate, which she should have left in September 1893. As a lay sister, Sr. Martha has to stay there four years.

PUBLICATION: HA 53, pp. 255f.

CIRCUMSTANCES: Some particular event must have been related to the Carmelites of Lisieux that affected Thérèse "painfully," but no one has been able to identify it.

SOURCES: To situate this prayer, it is interesting to put it in the great current of reparation that developed in the 19th century, still under the shock of the antireligious violence of the Revolution of 1789. Apart from being directed toward the Holy Trinity, this text has nothing in common with the widespread formulas of the time. In 1885 the child Thérèse was affiliated with the Archconfraternity of Reparation of Saint Dizier (1847) and the Confraternity of the Holy Face of Tours (1876). The first is dedicated to the Holy Trinity and the Holy Name of Jesus. Its insignia is a cross bearing on one side the radiating triangle (Trinity) and on the other the Holy Face; emblems, moreover, that we find on Thérèse's coat-of-arms (cf. Ms A, 86r). We know the important role played by M. Dupont, "the holy man of Tours," and by Sr. Mary of Saint Peter, also of Tours, in the development of the movement of reparation. The apparition of La Salette (September 19, 1846) could only strengthen this élan. Thérèse surely knew the little work: *Association de prières, contre le blasphème, les imprécations et la profanation des jours de dimanche et de fête* [Association of Prayers Against Blasphemies, Swearing, and Profanation of Sundays and Holy Days], under the patronage of St. Louis, King of France (Tours: Mame, 1847); also P. Janvier, *Vie de la Soeur Saint Pierre* (Tours, 1881) [translated as *Life of Sister Saint Peter* (Baltimore and New York: John Murphy & Co., 1885)] which was widely read at Lisieux. Often exploited without discretion against an apocalyptic background, these currents of piety favored the multiplication of "victims of the Justice of God" (Ms A, 84r). Cf. Pri 6.

NOTES

Nothing dramatic in Pri 4. Rather, it illustrates Psalm 8: Thérèse and her companion offer the "praise of children"—and their generosity—to exalt not only the Name of God but also his unappreciated love. The Carmelite associates creation with this praise, which she wants to be "harmonious" (concert, song, music, melody), adorned with beauty (diamonds, precious stones), sweet-smelling (fragrance of flowers). It is in the flowery style of her poem "Saint Cecilia" (PN 3) composed at the same time. While smiling and singing, Thérèse will "prove her love by works" (Ms B, 4r–v) in multiplying sacrifices. After her death, the novices will take up this method for a while (cf. Marie of the Eucharist, VT no. 99, p. 26).

Title: Like that of Pri 3, it must be authentic, for the copyist of 1910, Sr. Marie of the Child Jesus, is one of the most reliable.

Trinity: second of 27 mentions of the Trinity in the writings. Far beyond these references, and even if she is centered explicitly on the Person of Jesus, Thérèse is too much a disciple of St. John of the Cross not to live in an habitual Trinitarian atmosphere. The Act of Oblation well illustrates her Christian prayer, as she moves with ease from one Person to the other.

3: *blasphemies:* cf. PN 17.11 (*Poésies*, vol. 2, pp. 113f.); RP 2, 8r; Ms A, 52r; PN 24, 29. Note Thérèse's precocious maturity regarding blasphemers, brought out by Marcelline Husé who often took her to school: "I recall in particular how, even before her first communion, when we heard some workmen blaspheming, she excused them. She explained to me that we should not judge their inmost souls, for these men had received far fewer graces than we had and that they were unfortunate rather than blameworthy" (PO, 362). We should also point out her thoughtfulness toward the community when in the second Joan of Arc play she replaces "in God's name"—a familiar phrase with Joan—with "in my God" in order not to shock the sensibilities of her audience (cf. RP, p. 324). Thoughtful also in regard to her sisters and her prioress when in 1896–1897, she avoids speaking of the "dark thoughts" that obsess her (DE, pp. 525f.) for fear of "blaspheming" (Ms C, 7r). She doesn't even permit "imprecations" and scolds Sr. Geneviève sharply when she grumbles against God's ways in her regard. "Please! never any 'imprecations' " (CSG, p. 72; *Memoir*, p. 98; cf. *Association de Prières*, pp. 7, 43). For her there is only one attitude: "gratitude" (CSG, ibid.; Ms B, 1v = LT 196; Ms C, 25r, etc.) the precise antidote against every kind of blasphemy.

4: *to repair [réparer]:* this verb is found in LT 50 and 65; RP 1, 6v (subject: "God," the Word Incarnate); Pri 4 (3 times); RP 3, 16r; Pri 10; RP 8, 3v and 4r; Ms C, 7r; CJ 13.7.9; 20.7.1 (cf. 9.9.1).

8: *little birds:* sheet A lists, from Sunday to Saturday: "Dove, Nightingale, Warbler, Robin, Finch, Lark, Sparrow." In two weeks the "Number of all the melodies sung by the birds" (that is, the sacrifices of Thérèse and Martha) is 208.

9: *ingratitude:* because, with a God of Love, "everything is a grace" (CJ 5.6.4). Thérèse considers "ingratitude" what the heart of God "must feel the most" (LT 122). In her eyes, the "sinner," the "wicked," is first of all "ungrateful."

10–11: *musical instruments:* according to sheet A v: "Lyre, Harp, Violin, Accordion, Mandolin, Guitar, Flute." "Number of melodies": 84.

12: *melodious lyre:* Thérèse's favorite instrument, cf. RP 5, p. 357. The first version of PN 3 (composed at the same time) has for its title: "The Melody of St. Cecilia," dedicated to Céline, "the lyre of Jesus." On August 6, 1895, when composing "Notes of Reparation," Sr. Geneviève writes: "In my [Jesus'] Ears there resounds always the cry of blasphemers. I would like a soul to be occupied unceasingly in making me hear sweet harmonies."

13: *indifference:* another form of lack of love and thus of sin, in Thérèse's eyes; cf. LT 196: "Jesus meets only with the ungrateful and the indifferent"; RP 5, 1r ("profound indifference").

15: *precious stones:* according to sheet B r: "Diamonds, fine pearls, Rubies, Emeralds, Sapphires, Topazes, Hyacinths," for a total of 23 sacrifices. Like the lyre above, Thérèse has preference here for the "diamond" (recall that M. Martin, watchmaker-jeweler, nicknamed his daughters Marie and Pauline his "diamond" and "fine pearl").

15–19: *eagerness...worldly goods:* a probable allusion to work on Sunday, a profanation deplored by the Virgin of La Salette. In RP 6, Thérèse will come back to this problem of "passing riches"; cf. RP, p. 371.

18: *vigilant:* Sr. Martha related this advice of Thérèse: "Be vigilant [...]; if you knew what the price of a little act of renunciation was worth in the eyes of Jesus, you would seek them as eagerly as a miser seeks treasure" (PO, 429). Such, for her, is the "work" of the Carmelite.

20: *the fragrance of flowers:* according to sheet B v: "Lilies, Roses, Lilies of the Valley, Honeysuckle, Lilacs, Pinks, Violets." Total for the week: 27 sacrifices. As early as 1884, Sr. Agnes of Jesus initiated the child Thérèse in the symbolism of perfume. St. John of the Cross revealed to her all its mystical meaning; for example, *Spiritual Canticle,* 17.7–9; 24.6.

22–23: *priestly and religious souls:* one of the great concerns of Thérèse's prayer; cf. Ms A, 69v; letters to Céline (LT 94); RP 2, 7r; Pri 5, 3v, note; Pri 8 and 15.

24: *after the exile:* cf. Pri 6, 7, 12, 17. Far beyond the cliché (which is familiar to the Christian perspective; cf. the ending of the *Salve Regina*), the eschatological tendency of Thérèse's life and prayer is expressed here.

Attentive to banishing from her life all "ingratitude...indifference...offense...," Thérèse confirms this prayer in June 1897, when she writes at the end of her New Testament: "Lord, you fill me with joy for all that you do" (Ps 91 [92]). At that time she was suffering in body and soul and assailed by a spirit of blasphemy (cf. Ms C, 7r). This "cry of gratitude and love in the midst of trial" (C, 25r) is indeed the heroic refusal of even the appearance of blasphemy.

Prayer 5

"Mystical Flowers"

On the cover
> Madeleine! My Beloved Bride!
> I am all yours and you are all mine forever.

Title Page
1r   Mystical Flowers for my Bridal Bouquet.
        A voice is heard: "See the Bridegroom comes.
        Go out to meet Him...."(Gospel).

Aspirations
   (For the complete wording of each page, see below. We omit here mention of the day and the word "Aspirations," repeated seventeen times.)

2r   White Roses.
        O Jesus! purify my soul that it may become worthy
        to be your bride!

2v   Daisies.
        O Jesus! grant me the grace in all I do to please
        You alone.

3r   White Violets.
        Jesus, gentle and humble of Heart, make my heart
        like yours!...

3v   Lilies of the Valley.
        Saint Teresa, my Mother, teach me to save souls so
        that I may become a true Carmelite.

4r   Wild Roses.
O Jesus! it is you alone I serve when I serve my Mothers and Sisters.

4v   Tea Roses.
Jesus, Mary, Joseph, grant me the grace to make a good retreat and prepare my soul for the beautiful day of my profession.

5r   White Bellflowers.
O Saint Mary Magdalene! obtain for me the grace that my life may be one act of love.

5v   Honeysuckle.
O Jesus! teach me to deny myself always to please my sisters.

6r   White Periwinkles.
My God, I love you with all my heart.

6v   White Peonies.
O my God, look at the Face of Jesus and count all sinners among the elect.

7r   Jasmine.
O Jesus, I want to have joy only in You alone!...

7v   White Forget-me-nots.
O my Holy Guardian Angel! cover me always with your wings so that I may never have the misfortune to offend Jesus.

8r   Meadowsweet.*
               O Mary, my dear Mother, grant me the grace never
               to stain the robe of innocence that you will give me
               on the day of my profession.

8v   White Verbena.
               My God, I believe in you, I hope in you, I love you
               with all my heart.

9r   White Iris.
               My God, I thank you for all the graces you have
               given me during my retreat.

9r   The Great Day Has Arrived.
               Lilies.
               My Beloved Jesus, you are now all mine and I am
               your little Bride forever!!!.....

* in French "Reine des Prés" [Queen of the Meadows].

DOCUMENT: A notebook 10 x 8.3 cm, kept in an envelope on which Mother
    Agnes has written: "Little copybook written by Sr. Thérèse of the Child
    Jesus to prepare Sr. Marie-Madeleine for her profession." Light blue
    cardboard cover with photo vignette: "The life of Union" (Boumard, p.
    319). Text and arabesques are in blue ink. Five double sheets are at-
    tached to the cover with a blue ribbon.

1r: Title page, calligraphy in Gothic lettering, black ink (the same as that
    of RP 2, cf. RP, p. 302). Arabesques in blue ink. Oval vignette of Thérèse:
    this charcoal drawing by Sr. Geneviève was glued on some years later.

9r: the words: "I thank You" have been cut off, to be glued on an illumina-
    tion given to Pius XI on October 21, 1924. They wished to thank him
    for having dispensed from Gregorian chant the Carmels who preferred
    to keep to the *recto tono*. Cf. the brochure edited at that time by the
    Carmel of Lisieux: "In favor of the traditional recitation tone of the
    Carmelites." The illumination is reproduced at the end.

DATE: For November 20, 1894, but completed in October.

Composed for: Sr. Marie-Madeleine, a laysister novice, who entered July 22, 1892 and received the habit September 7, 1893. First professed nun of Mother Agnes and very attached to her, she avoided Thérèse, who was too perceptive for her taste. On these difficult relations, cf. CG II, pp. 728 and 924; presentation of PN 10 ("Story of a Shepherdess who became a Queen"); RP 7, notes; PO, 477–482.

Copy: CE IV, 71r–72r, at the end of the volume of *Poésies.* Title: "Little Collection of Aspirations composed by the Servant of God for the preparation of one of her novices, a lay sister named Marie-Madeleine of the Blessed Sacrament" (Correction: the mistress of novices is really Mother Marie de Gonzague). Copyist: Sr. Madeleine of Jesus.

Publication: Unpublished text, except for scattered quotes in CG, PN, and BT. The document is not even mentioned in Mss I, pp. 20–29.

NOTES

Obliged to be very discreet in regard to her rather touchy companion, Thérèse offers her a most modest collection. It follows exactly the schema of the one Sr. Agnes prepared in 1884 for Thérèse's first communion (authentic text of the latter is in VT no. 76, October 1979, pp. 310ff). For the novice's "Wedding Basket" she keeps only white flowers—from "White Roses" (2r) to "Lilies" (9v)—set off by a touch of gold— "Tea Roses" (4v) and "Honeysuckle" (5v). Marie-Madeleine will pick 180 flowers (= sacrifices) in two weeks.

Aspirations: some bear Thérèse's mark (2v, 3v, 5r–v, 7v, 8r) but the rest are conventional. The novice has a total of 2,924, probably recited in series, like the decades of the rosary. (In 1884, Thérèse said 2,773 in two months and nine days.)

Cover: *My Bride...for ever:* cf. Song 2:16.

1r: *Mystical:* a rare adjective with Thérèse (Ms A, 79r; PN 54.7; and here). "A voice ... of Him": Mt 25:6.

3v: *save souls:* Thérèse tries to share with her companions her "ardent zeal for souls, especially for priests." Sister Marie-Madeleine quotes these words at the Process: "God will ask us for an accounting of the priests whom we could have saved by our prayers and our sacrifices but did not because of our infidelity and our laziness. Let us not lose a single one of our little sacrifices for them" (PO, 478).

3v: *true Carmelite:* cf. "A Carmelite who would not be an apostle would cease to be a daughter of the Seraphic Saint Teresa" (LT 198); see also LC 145.

4r: *You alone I serve:* cf. PN 10.7. Tactful allusion to Marie-Madeleine's condition as a laysister (cf. RP, p. 167).

4v: *a good retreat:* in order to have ten full days before profession, according to custom, the novice did not begin her retreat until Friday evening, November 9th.

6v: *O my God...among your elect:* according to an oral tradition handed down by Sister Geneviève, Thérèse said at the elevation of the host at Mass, and made the other novices say: "Holy Father, look on the Face of your Jesus and make all sinners the elect." She got this inspiration from a circular from the Guard of Honor of the Sacred Heart of Jesus: "The soul, mediatrix with the Sacred Heart" (1st series, 19th office): "Holy Father, look at the face of Jesus / And make all sinners among the elect!" These slips were drawn by lot on the first Friday of each month at the Carmel of Lisieux during Thérèse's time. We also know that at the elevation of the chalice, Thérèse said: "O Divine Blood of Jesus, water our earth, make the elect spring forth!", taking her inspiration from Sister Mary of Saint Peter (cf. *Life,* p. 341). Thérèse will write this prayer on a picture painted for P. Roulland (August 20, 1896) and will replace "earth" with "mission."

8r: *robe of innocence:* cf. Pri 2, 1–2. In 1897, shortly before her profession, Sister Marie of the Eucharist wrote her parents: "God himself will pardon all the faults of my life and when you see me again you will be able to contemplate in my soul the same innocence I had when I was washed in the waters of Baptism as a little child" (March 13, 1897).

Prayer 6

Act of Oblation to Merciful Love

J. M. J. T.
Offering of myself as a Victim of Holocaust
to God's Merciful Love

O My God! Most Blessed Trinity, I desire [5]to *Love* you and make you Loved, to work for the glory of Holy Church by saving souls on earth and liberating those suffering in purgatory. I desire to accomplish your will perfectly and to reach the degree of glory [10]you have prepared for me in your kingdom. I desire, in a word, to be a Saint, but I feel my helplessness and I beg you, O my God! to be yourself my Sanctity!

Since You loved me so much as to give me [15]your only Son as my Savior and my Spouse, the infinite treasures of his merits are mine. I offer them to you with gladness, begging you to look on me only through the Face of Jesus and in his Heart burning with Love.

[20]I offer you, too, all the merits of the Saints (in Heaven and on earth), their acts of Love, and those of the Holy Angels. Finally, I offer you, O Blessed Trinity! the Love and merits of the Blessed Virgin, my dear Mother. It is to her [25]I abandon my offering, begging her to present it to you. Her Divine Son, my Beloved Spouse, told us in the days of his mortal life: "Whatsoever you ask the Father in my name he will give it to you!" I am certain, then, that you will grant my desires; I [30]know, O my God! That the more you want to give, the more you make us desire. I feel in my

heart immense desires and it is with confidence I ask you
to come and take possession of my soul. Ah! I cannot receive Holy Communion as often as I desire, but, Lord, are
you not All-Powerful? Remain in me as in a tabernacle and
never separate yourself from your little host......

[35]I want to console you for the ingratitude of the
wicked, and I beg of you to take away my freedom to displease you. If through weakness I sometimes fall, may your
Divine Glance cleanse my soul immediately, consuming all
my imperfections like the fire that transforms everything
into itself......

I thank you, O my God! for all the graces you have
granted me, especially the grace [40]of making me pass
through the crucible of suffering. It is with joy I shall contemplate You on the last day carrying the scepter of your
Cross. Since you deigned to give me a share in this very
precious Cross, I hope in Heaven to resemble you and to
see shining in my glorified body the sacred stigmata of
Your Passion...

After earth's exile, I hope to go and enjoy you in the
Fatherland, but I do not want [45]to lay up merits for Heaven.
I want to work for your Love alone with the one purpose of
pleasing you, consoling your Sacred Heart, and saving
souls who will love you eternally.

In the evening of this life, I shall appear before you
with empty hands, for I do not ask you, Lord, to count my
works. All our justice is stained in your eyes. [50]I wish, then,
to be clothed in your own Justice and to receive from your
Love the eternal possession of Yourself. I want no other
Throne, no other Crown but You, my Beloved!......

Time is nothing in your eyes, and a single day is like a
thousand years; you can, then, in one instant prepare me
to appear before you...

[55]In order to live in one single act of perfect Love, I offer myself as a victim of holocaust to your merciful love, asking you to consume me incessantly, allowing the waves of infinite tenderness shut up within you to overflow into my soul, and that thus I may become [60]a Martyr of your Love, O my God!...

May this martyrdom, after having prepared me to appear before you, finally cause me to die and may my soul take its flight without any delay into the eternal embrace of Your Merciful [65]Love...

I want, O my Beloved, at each beat of my heart to renew this offering to you an infinite number of times, until the shadows having disappeared [70]I may be able to tell you of my Love in an Eternal Face to Face!...

Marie, Françoise, Thérèse of the Child Jesus
and the Holy Face
unworthy Carmelite religious

[75]Feast of the Most Holy Trinity
The 9th day of June in the year of grace 1895.

DOCUMENTS

There are 3 autographs of the Act of Oblation:

Loose sheet A: written June 9–11, 1895. A facsimile of it was reproduced in the "Appended Pieces" of the photocopy edition of the *Manuscrits autobiographiques*, 1956.

Loose sheet B: an incomplete transcription (8 lines) probably at the end of 1896. The original is in the possession of the Missionary Brothers of Saint Thérèse in Bassac (Charente).

Loose sheet C: written for Mother Agnes at the end of 1896 or beginning of 1897. It is kept in a reliquary at the Carmel. Since 1902 it has been circulated in facsimile. This is the version our edition uses.

Definitive Version (Sheet C)

Afd, about 6.7 x 11 cm (the part visible in the reliquary measures 13.2 x 10.9 cm). Very fine handwriting, in which the writing alternates between upright and slanted; some words are enlarged. Inside the sheet the writing extends continuously across 1v and 2r. Another hand has emphasized and sometimes corrected the punctuation and accents.

Other Versions

Sheet A

Afs 20.4 x 13 cm, 4 x 4 graph paper, yellowed, torn at the corners; folded in four and worn at the crease mark, reinforced with gummed paper. Thérèse redid and rewrote the lower left-hand corner (about 6 x 2.4 cm); the handwriting indeed seems to be that of June 1897. At the upper left-hand corner there is a scorch mark: "It comes from an accident. P. Lemonnier apologized, he had held the precious sheet too close to his candle." On this testimony of Mother Agnes of Jesus, cf. p. 63. Most of the numerous erasures and corrections on this sheet could date from the year 1896.

6–7: *finally, my God, I would like to make myself worthy of my vocation by helping your apostles to win all hearts for You:* interlinear addition between lines 5–6 and 6–7, repeated on sheet B and then scratched out with pencil. The addition could date from the end of 1896.

13: *and in His Heart burning with Love:* interlinear addition; suggested by Sr. Marie of the Sacred Heart (probably summer of 1895).

20: *immense:* written over the scratched out word. First version had "infinite"; correction asked for by P. Lemonnier, cf. below.

35–36: *to console your Sacred Heart by saving souls who will love you eternally:* interlinear addition that Sr. Marie of the Sacred Heart requested.

Mother Agnes's envelope

Later, this loose sheet A was put away in a small grey-blue envelope (74 x 113 mm) on which Mother Agnes later wrote: "First text of the Act of Love written by our little Thérèse to be submitted to P. Lemonnier, missionary of La Délivrande. He approved it but asked for a small correction that our Saint made on this rough draft. She wore it over her heart and made a beautifully encased copy of it for me. The scorch mark comes from an accident. P. Lemonnier apologized. He had held the precious sheet too close to his candle.

Sr. Agnes of Jesus"

Offrande de moi-même, comme Victime d'Holocauste
à l'Amour Miséricordieux du Bon Dieu.

O mon Dieu! Trinité Bienheureuse, je désire vous Aimer et vous faire Aimer, travailler pour la glorification de la Sainte Église en sauvant les âmes qui sont sur la terre et en délivrant celles qui souffrent dans le purgatoire [...] Je désire accomplir parfaitement votre Volonté et arriver au degré de gloire que vous m'avez préparé dans votre royaume en un mot je désire être Sainte, mais je sens mon impuissance et je vous demande, ô mon Dieu, d'être vous-même ma Sainteté. Puisque vous m'avez aimée, jusqu'à me donner votre Fils unique pour être mon Sauveur et mon Époux, les trésors infinis de ses mérites sont à moi, je vous les offre avec bonheur, vous suppliant de ne me regarder qu'à travers la Face de Jésus [...] Je vous offre encore tous les mérites des Saints, leurs actes d'amour et ceux des Anges, enfin je vous offre, ô Bienheureuse Trinité, les mérites de la Sainte Vierge [...] c'est à elle que j'abandonne mon offrande, la priant de vous la présenter. Son Divin Fils [...] jours de sa vie mortelle nous a dit: «Tout ce que vous demanderez à mon Père en mon nom il vous le donnera». Je suis donc certaine que vous exaucerez mes désirs, je le sais, ô mon Dieu, plus vous voulez donner, plus vous faites désirer. Je sens en mon cœur des désirs immenses et c'est avec confiance que je vous demande de venir prendre possession de mon âme. Ah! je ne puis recevoir la Ste Communion aussi souvent que je le désire, mais, Seigneur n'êtes-vous pas Tout-Puissant? Restez en moi comme au tabernacle, ne vous éloignez jamais de votre petite hostie....
Je voudrais vous consoler de l'ingratitude des méchants et je vous supplie de m'ôter la liberté de vous déplaire, si par faiblesse je tombe quelquefois que aussitôt votre Divin Regard purifie mon âme, consumant toutes mes imperfections comme le feu qui transforme toute chose en lui-même.........
Je vous remercie, ô mon Dieu, de toutes les grâces que vous m'avez accordées en particulier de m'avoir fait passer par le creuset de la souffrance, c'est avec joie que je vous contemplerai au dernier jour portant le sceptre de la Croix, puisque vous avez daigné me donner en partage cette Croix si précieuse, j'espère au ciel, vous ressembler et voir briller sur mon corps glorifié les sacrés stigmates de votre Passion...... Après l'exil de la terre, j'espère aller jouir de vous dans la Patrie, mais je ne veux pas amasser de mérites pour le ciel, je veux travailler pour votre seul Amour, dans l'unique but de vous faire plaisir, de consoler votre Cœur Sacré [...] Au soir de la vie, je paraîtrai devant vous les mains vides, car je ne vous demande pas, Seigneur, de compter mes œuvres. Toutes nos justices ont des taches à vos yeux, je veux donc me revêtir de votre propre Justice et recevoir de votre Amour la possession éternelle de Vous-Même, je ne veux point d'autre trône et d'autre couronne que Vous, ô mon Bien Aimé!......
A vos yeux, le temps n'est rien un seul jour est comme mille ans, vous pouvez donc en un instant me préparer à paraître devant vous......

Pri 6: Act of Oblation to Merciful Love (loose sheet A, recto)

Afin de vivre dans un acte de parfait Amour, Je m'offre comme Victime d'Holocauste à votre Amour Miséricordieux, vous suppliant de me consumer sans cesse, laissant déborder en mon âme les flots de tendresse infinie qui sont renfermés en vous et qu'ainsi je devienne Martyre de votre Amour ô mon Dieu!.......

Que ce martyre après m'avoir préparée à paraître devant vous me fasse enfin mourir et que mon âme s'élance sans retard dans l'Éternel embrassement de Votre Miséricordieux Amour!

Je veux ô mon Bien-Aimé, à chaque battement de mon cœur vous renouveler cette offrande un nombre infini de fois, jusqu'à ce que les ombres s'étant évanouies et qu'alors je puisse vous redire mon Amour dans un Face à Face éternel!........

M. Fse. Thérèse de l'Enfant Jésus de la Ste Face
rel. carm. ind.

Fête de la Très Sainte Trinité.
Dimanche 9 Juin 1895

Pri 6: Act of Oblation to Merciful Love (loose sheet A, verso)

The correction asked for was to replace "infinite" (20)with "immense." Let us note also that it was not a "rough draft" but a very carefully made copy that was sent free of any mistakes or changes, probably in June or July 1895, to P. Lemonnier, although he speaks of October (cf. PO, 580 and 582, and below).

SHEET B

Afd identical in paper and format to sheet C. The reproduction on the back of the cover of the *Annals* of July–August 1952 is quite enlarged. This is the text, which consists of 8 lines:

O my God! Blessed Trinity, I desire to love you and to make you loved, to work for the glory of Holy Church by saving souls who are on earth and delivering those who suffer in purgatory. Finally, my God, I would like to make myself worthy of my vocation by helping your apostles to conquer all hearts for you.

We do not know for whom this unfinished text was destined. The handwriting is very close to that of sheet C and does seem to be related to it. Among other possible hypotheses we may think that on reflection, Thérèse must have judged it best not to retain the phrase on the apostolate; or that it is a question of a preliminary version on paper for the copy intended for Mother Agnes of Jesus. Placed in a reliquary and authenticated by Mother Agnes of Jesus and Sr. Geneviève, this autograph was offered to P. Martin, Superior of the Diocesan Missionaries of Vendée, for his priestly jubilee in January 1947. It is in the possession of the Missionary Brothers of Saint Thérèse.

DATE

The text of sheet A was composed between June 9 and 11, 1895. Copies B and C are probably from the end of 1896 or the beginning of 1897.

WRITTEN FOR HERSELF AND SISTER GENEVIÈVE

The essence of Thérèse's offering was made without formulated phrases, in a few words, during Mass on June 9, 1895. But from the beginning she foresaw that this Act of Oblation would be communicated to others, and first to her sister Céline. Hence she needed to compose a text that could be submitted for authorization by her superiors.

COPIES

MSC Copy: an early copy has been found (probably from the summer of 1895) drawn up by Sr. Marie of the Sacred Heart. It is a sheet identical to sheet A (20.4 x 13 cm); folded in four and again in three; it is kept in a small brown leather case and is in very poor condition. This copy is of the greatest critical interest, for it reproduces sheet A before any corrections (with the exception of a slip in line 9: "see" instead of the word "feel" of sheets A and C). Only later will Sister Marie of the Sacred Heart write on her copy the interlinear additions pointed out in the description of sheet A, and other revisions. Thus we reproduce this copy, free of any correction, for it probably represents the original text Thérèse read in the presence of Sister Geneviève on June 11 (we italicize the two variants of this text that we will mention below):

J. M. J. T.

Offering of myself as a Victim of Holocaust to God's Merciful Love

O My God! Most Blessed Trinity, I desire to love you and to make you loved, to work for the glory of Holy Church by saving souls on earth and liberating those suffering in purgatory. I desire to accomplish your will perfectly and to reach the degree of glory You have prepared for me in your kingdom. I desire, in a word, to be a Saint but I see my helplessness and I beg you, O my God, to be Yourself my Sanctity. Since you loved me so much as to give me your only Son as my Savior and my Spouse, the infinite treasures of his merits are mine. I offer them to you gladly, begging you to look upon me only through the Face of Jesus. I offer you, too, all the merits of the Saints, their acts of love and those of the Angels. Finally, I offer you, O Blessed Trinity, the merits of the Blessed Virgin. It is to her I abandon my offering, begging her to present it to you. Her divine Son told us in the days of his mortal life: "Whatsoever you ask the Father in my name he will give it to you." I am certain, then, that you will grant my desires. I feel it, O my God, the more you want to give, the more you make us desire. I feel within me *immense* desires and it is with confidence I ask you to come and take possession of my soul. Ah! I cannot receive Holy Communion as often as I desire, but are you not Almighty?.. Remain in me as in a tabernacle and never separate yourself from your little victim... I want to console you for the ingratitude of the wicked, and I beg of you to take away my freedom to displease you. If through weakness I may sometimes fall, may your divine Glance cleanse my soul immediately, consuming all my imperfections like the fire that transforms everything into itself...

[v] I thank you, O my God, for all the graces you have granted me, especially the grace of making me pass through the crucible of suffering. It is with joy I shall contemplate you on the last day carrying the scepter of the Cross. Since you deigned to give me a share in this very precious Cross, I hope in heaven to resemble you and to see shining in my glorified body the sacred stigmata of your Passion... After earth's exile, I hope to go and enjoy you in the Fatherland, but I do not want to lay up merits for Heaven. I want to work for your Love alone with the one purpose of pleasing you, *of consoling Your Sacred Heart.*

In the evening of life, I shall appear before you with empty hands, for I do not ask you, Lord, to count my works. All our justice is stained in your eyes. I wish to be clothed in your own Justice and to receive from your Love the eternal possession of Yourself. I want no other throne, no other crown but You, O my Beloved... Time is nothing in your eyes, and a single day is like a thousand years. You can, then, in one instant prepare me to appear before you...

In order to live in an act of perfect Love, I offer myself as a Victim of holocaust to your merciful Love, asking you to consume me incessantly, allowing the waves of infinite tenderness shut up within you to overflow into my soul, and that thus I may become a martyr of your Love, O my God... May this martyrdom, after having prepared me to appear before you, finally cause me to die and may my soul take its flight without any delay into the eternal embrace of Your Merciful Love!...

I want, O my Beloved, at each beat of my heart to renew this offering to you an infinite number of times, until the shadows wane and then I may be able to tell you of my love in an eternal face to face...

Marie of the Sacred Heart
unworthy Carmelite religious

Feast of the Most Blessed Trinity
Sunday, June 9,1895

We have italicized "immense" written over the crossed-out word "infinite." Beyond doubt this correction was made at the very time of the copy, for the word "immense" is enlarged and in the same color ink as the rest. Perhaps Marie has before her eyes the word "infinite," but when Thérèse lent her her copy, she urged her to put "immense," as P. Lemonnier had just advised. As for the addition, "of consoling your Sacred Heart," perhaps Marie did this on her own initiative. It is in the same ink and same handwriting as the rest. Perhaps she pointed it out to Thérèse when she returned her copy to her and Thérèse adopted it, even adding to it the mentions of the Sacred Heart. We will say more about these additions later.

Copy of the Writings

In CE II, 178r–179v, the copyist, Marie of the Child Jesus, very faithfully follows sheet C by alternating straight and slanted writing.

PUBLICATION

Text published since HA 98, pp. 257ff., according to loose sheet C. Variant: "If I should fall through weakness."

CIRCUMSTANCES

Now that we have all of Thérèse's writings, we can better discern her spiritual itinerary. We know in particular how in October 1894, Thérèse discovered the main themes indispensable to her little way: childhood and mercy (cf. RP, pp. 90 and 302). The retrospective glance she casts over her life when writing her autobiography (Ms A) convinces her that it is only her littleness that drew Mercy toward her. Likewise, she teaches Marie of the Trinity that "the only way to make rapid progress in the way of love is to remain little" (CSM no. 31). In the spring of 1895, Thérèse knew she was ill, that she had no more than "two or three years left" (PO, 399). Love alone can "consume her rapidly," according to the expression of Saint John of the Cross.

Victims of Divine Justice

At the end of 1895, in her Manuscript A, Thérèse comes back to the inspiration of June 9, 1895 (which, Sister Geneviève tells us, took place during the Eucharist). "I was thinking," she wrote, "about the souls who offer themselves as victims of God's Justice in order to turn away the punishments reserved to sinners, drawing them upon themselves" (Ms A, 84r). Of whom was Thérèse thinking? Names have been suggested: Sister Marie of the Cross (1812–1882) or Mother Geneviève of Saint Teresa (1805–1891), both foundresses of the Carmel of Lisieux. But their offering as "victims" does not correspond to what Thérèse aims for here. Neither does her own father's offering. What we did not know till now is that the French Carmels saw a hundred Carmelites die in 1894–1895. Thus, nearly that many obituary circulars were read in the refectory. Nothing is more instructive than this Carmelite literature, unexplored to this day. We might wonder if, on June 9, 1895, Thérèse was not thinking more particularly of Sister Marie of Jesus, Carmelite of Luçon, whose obituary circular had just arrived at Lisieux on June 8. It revealed that this sister "often offered herself as a victim to Divine Justice." Her death agony on Good Friday, 1895, was terrible. The dying nun let this cry of anguish escape: "I bear the rigors of divine Justice... divine Justice!...divine Justice!..." And again: "I do not have enough merits. I must acquire them." The account is impressive and could have struck its listeners.

"How much more your Love..." (Ms A, 84r)

If Thérèse refuses to let herself be closed up in the dialectic "God of wrath or God of love?" (cf. RP, p. 89), if she does not have to choose mercy *rather* than justice, which, "perhaps this even more so than the others (divine perfections) seemed to her clothed in love" (Ms A, 83v), her reaction is no less clear: "From the depths of my heart, I cried out: 'O my God! Will Your Justice alone find souls willing to immolate themselves as victims? Does not Your Merciful Love need them too? On every side this love is unknown, rejected; those hearts upon whom You would lavish it turn to creatures seeking happiness from them with their miserable affection; they do this instead of throwing themselves into Your arms and of accepting Your infinite Love. O my God! Is Your disdained Love going to remain closed up within Your Heart? It seems to me that if You were to find souls offering themselves as victims of holocaust to Your Love, You would consume them rapidly; it seems to me too, that You would be happy not to hold back the waves of infinite tenderness within You. If Your Justice loves to release itself, this Justice which extends only over the earth, how much more does Your Merciful Love desire to set souls on fire since Your Mercy reaches to the heavens. O my Jesus, let me be this happy victim; consume Your holocaust with the fire of Your Divine Love!...' " (Ms A, 84).

"On coming out of this unforgettable Mass," Sister Geneviève relates, "she confided to me what she had just done and the grace she had received" (NPPO 1908, p. 46). In a more explicit text, Sister Geneviève expresses herself thus: "It was June 9, Feast of the Holy Trinity. On coming out of Mass, her eyes were shining and she was breathing a holy enthusiasm. Without saying a word, Thérèse took me to find Our Mother, who at that time was Mother Agnes of Jesus. She recounted to her in my presence how she had just offered herself as a Victim of Holocaust to Merciful Love, and she asked permission for us to offer ourselves together. Our Mother, who was very busy at the time, gave permission for everything without understanding too well what it was all about. Once we were alone Thérèse confided to me the grace she had received and she began to compose an act of offering that we officially pronounced together two days later on June 11" (Intimate Souvenirs, 1909, pp. 269f.; unedited text).

Permission for both of us (PA, 280)

For Thérèse, then, it was done. She surrendered to Merciful Love in the secret of her heart during the Mass of June 9. But she knew already that this grace was not for her alone. Once again, let us listen to Sister Geneviève: "When we came out of Mass, she drew me after her to go look for our Mother. She seemed as if in a daze and did not speak to me. When we finally found our Mother [Agnes of Jesus] she asked her for permission to offer herself with me as a victim of merciful Love and gave her a short explanation. Our Mother was busy and did not seem to understand too well what it was all about but gave permission for everything, such was her confidence in the discretion of Sister Thérèse of the Child Jesus" (PO, 281). Thus, the requested permission focused on offering herself "with" Sister Geneviève. She admitted: "I did not understand, it is true, the whole meaning of the act I made, but I had full confidence in the inspirations of my dear Thérèse and desired to surrender myself as she did and in the same measure as she. After this gift to Love, my union with Jesus became closer still" (Intimate Souvenirs, 1909, *loc. cit.*). After Mass on June 9, then, Thérèse told Céline that "she would gather her thoughts together on paper" (CSG, p. 67; *Memoir,* p. 89). On this Sunday, no special duty occupied her; her time was free. Perhaps she wrote a rough draft (which has disappeared), for loose sheet A is very carefully drawn up. The two sisters met on Tuesday, June 11, kneeling before the statue of the Virgin of the Smile to offer themselves "together."

The examination of a theologian

When Mother Agnes of Jesus recalled during the Process the circumstances of the Offering to Love, she stated: "Then, she composed the formula of her gift and submitted it to me. She also expressed the idea of submitting it to a theologian for examination. It was Père Lemonnier, superior of the Missionaries of *La Déliverande*, who examined it. He answered simply that there was nothing in it contrary to faith, however, she should not say 'I feel within me infinite desires' but 'I feel within me immense desires.' This was a sacrifice for the Servant of God; however, she did it without any complaint. Besides, the substance was approved and she showed much joy at this" (PO, 158).

We can reestablish the facts as follows: a few days after June 11, 1895, Mother Agnes of Jesus sent Thérèse's copy (sheet A) to Père Armand Lemonnier, who had already given the community retreats in October

1893 and 1894, and did so again in October 1895. Thérèse herself did not write; Sister Geneviève told her spiritual director at that time (the same P. Lemonnier) of her happiness at offering herself to merciful Love. For more security, P. Lemonnier consulted his superior and namesake (PO, 582 and PA, 104). A little later, he doubtless gave directly to Mother Agnes the response indicated above, and he answered Sister Geneviève by a letter (which she dated as June) encouraging her in this way of being a victim of love (cf. CG II, p. 808). Happy at this approval, Thérèse enrolled a new disciple.

The offering of Marie of the Sacred Heart (summer 1895)

Later, Marie recalled the circumstances of her own offering: "During June 1895, some days after she had offered herself to Merciful Love, I was working in the garden with her [drying the hay]. She asks me: 'Would you like to make the Act of Offering to Merciful Love? — I don't know what you mean, I told her, for I had not yet heard her speak of it. — Very well! she answered, you know that there are souls who offer themselves as victims to the Justice of God. Oh yes, I answered right away but I do not care very much for such things.'

Then Sister Thérèse explained to me very simply that it was not a question of offering oneself to the Justice of God but rather to his Merciful Love. Then you will see, she concluded, you have nothing to fear, for from this Love one can expect only Mercy. I let her give me this Act, just as she had just composed it, but I reserved for myself the right to reflect on it more before making it. When I had read it, I remarked to her that there was no mention of the Sacred Heart in it. It was to please me that she then added: 'Begging You to look upon me only through the Face of Jesus *and in His Heart burning with love.*' Then, further on: 'I want to work for Your Love alone with the one purpose of pleasing You, *consoling Your Sacred Heart* and saving souls who will love You eternally' " (Cited in Mss II, pp. 59f.).

The offering of Marie of the Trinity (December 1, 1895)

A few months passed. Next, on November 30, 1895, Thérèse spoke of her Offering to her novice, Sister Marie of the Trinity. Enthusiastic, then hesitant, the novice made this Act on December 1. (The account of it is in CSM no. 38, VT, no. 77, January 1980, with references to various parallel accounts that the witness made of it).

Mother Agnes of Jesus

To one of her daughters who questioned her on this subject (after 1922), Mother Agnes confessed that she had adopted the Offering to Love so late that she didn't even want to mention the date. Be that as it may, she accepted the definitive copy from Thérèse—loose sheet C—and integrated all the revisions of detail added after P. Lemonnier's approval. This loose sheet was edited in facsimile from 1902 on.

An offering actualized

The questions and objections of the first disciples, and especially her own spiritual experience that was in constant progress, led Thérèse to specify the content and meaning of her offering. We should reread in this light her September 1896 conversation with Marie of the Sacred Heart: Ms B, 2nd part (2r–5v) which is of September 8; Marie's letter (LC 169); Ms B, 1r–v (= LT 196); Marie's new letter (LC 170), and finally the letter called "charter for little souls," LT 197. These texts bring this fact to light: the offering to Love is the act of a child, of a poor one. On the one hand, "mercy is granted to little ones" (cf. LT 196); on the other, "the only road that leads to this divine furnace [=the holocaust of merciful Love], and this road is the *abandonment* of the little child who sleeps without fear in his Father's arms..." (LT 196). It is confidence [of a child] and nothing but confidence that must lead us to Love!" (LT 197). She ends her Manuscript B with this phrase: "Jesus ... I beg You to choose a legion of little Victims worthy of Your LOVE." Spiritual childhood and holocaust of merciful Love are from now on linked indissolubly in her doctrine.

SOURCES

Borne along by a great inspiration, Thérèse had no need of "sources" to compose her act of offering. She draws from the new and the old of the treasure in her heart, a treasure she had received in its essentials from the church and from her Order.

Liturgy: The feast of June 9 certainly accentuated the Trinitarian coloring of the text. The evening before, they read in the refectory the translation of the Divine Office. The invocation "O Blessed Trinity" is repeated in it like a leitmotif. As for the Mass itself, the entrance, offertory, and communion chants bless the Holy Trinity "because it has treated us mercifully."

Scripture: Biblical quotations have their place in this prayer, as we would expect.

Saint John of the Cross: Thérèse is remembering—more by saturation than erudition—the *Spiritual Canticle* and the *Living Flame of Love*. A rereading of the Offering to Love in the light of the writings of John of the Cross may open surprising insights.

Circulars: We have pointed out the seminal role played by the obituary notice of Sister Marie of Jesus and the interest of the other French Carmelite circulars (more than 500 Carmelites died during Thérèse's religious life).

NOTES AND COMMENTARY

The Act of Oblation has occasioned countless exegeses. We will make almost no allusion to them in the following notes: we limit ourselves to clarifying Thérèse by Thérèse. The numbering of the lines is that of sheet C.

I. THE TITLE (1–3)

The title announces the precise object of the offering, in response to an inspiration of June 9, 1895. It is repeated in the text in the active form: "I offer myself as a victim of holocaust to Your Merciful Love." Thérèse never speaks of an "Act of Offering," the title that appears from HA 98, p. 257 on; and still less of "donation," a word absent from her writings.

1: *Offering:* a word repeated in lines 25 and 68; it appears when she recalls her important dates: "Offering of myself to Love" (Ms A, 86r); in the infirmary: "my offering to Love" (CJ 29.7.9) "my offering" (8.8.2). See also Ms A, 84r; RP, p. 338.

1–2: *Victim of Holocaust:* Thérèse received a thorough religious education and certainly knows the different forms of sacrifices in the Old Testament. She refers to this explicitly in Ms B, 3v: sacrifices "in times past." Possibly she is recalling here Wis 3:6 with its two possible translations: "host of holocaust," according to Le Maitre de Sacy, which she uses in RP 3, 19v, and the memorial card of M. Martin (BT, pp. 117 and 292): and "victim of holocaust," according to Bourassé and Janvier, the version Céline followed in her own scriptural notebook and in the one she copied for Thérèse; cf. VT no. 79, July 1980, p. 222. Keep in mind this equivalence host/victim; cf. *infra,* 1.34. In June 1895, Thérèse prefers "victim of holocaust" as a response to "victims of divine Justice" (Ms A, 84r). Note also the traditional assimilation of religious consecration to a "holocaust"; it is frequent in Thérèse's time. Cf. Sister Marie of the Angels: "Make yourself more and more a little host, a holocaust for Jesus" (LC 145 in CG II, p. 631; where Mother Marie de Gonzague writes: "My Léonie, the holocaust must be total to keep nothing for ourselves, to give *all* to Jesus" (Postscript to LT 173, January 1895).

2: *Merciful Love:* first appearance of the expression as such in her Writings; cf. also 1.56 and 64; Ms A, 84r (3x); Pri 10.10; LT 197; LT 261 and 262. In all these references it concerns the "Merciful Love" of Jesus.

II. 4–13: "O My God!...My Sanctity"

The first paragraph explains the purpose of the offering and develops in advance the "in order to" (55) of the final part. Thérèse lists her fundamental desires in it (compare with those of her Profession Note, Pri 2) and sums them up "in a word...Sanctity."

4: *Blessed Trinity:* cf. Pri 4.23; LT 183; PN 29.3; Ms B, 5v. The invocation appears often in the Office of the feast. By preferring it to "holy" or "adorable" (adjectives present in the same Office or in Thérèse's writings), she deliberately gives a joyful coloring to her offering.

4–5: *to love You and to make You Loved:* the complete formula—with a few variants—is already found in LT 96 (P. Pichon's letter, LC 126, only echoes it) and LT 114. We will find it again in LT 201, 206, 218, 220 (2 times), 225, 254. For the expression "to make loved," cf. LT 109; Pri 8.16; PN 24.26; PN 47.6; LT 221, 224, 226. In February 1897, Thérèse will write: " I shall desire in heaven the same thing as I do on earth: to love Jesus and to make Him loved" (LT 220). Thus, on this June 9 she expresses her basic *raison d'être* in response to the appeal of Jesus who "desires to be loved" (Ms A, 84r). The liturgical feast requires that she unite it with the heart of the Trinity but so also does her own spiritual experience which is ever more explicit; cf. PN 17, st. 1 and 2.

5 (and 45): *to work:* i.e., for Thérèse, to pray and sacrifice herself; cf. LT 71, 82, 95; Pri 4.2; Ms A, 45v; Pri 8.7; LT 189, 201, 213 (2 x), 220 (2 x), 221, 224; Ms C, 8v; LT 254.

5–6: *glory of Holy Church:* cf. PN 17.10. The very vivid sense of church was bequeathed by Teresa of Avila to her Order. Thérèse gives a primarily spiritual meaning to this "glory" (sole use of the word).

6–7: *saving...earth:* Thérèse entered Carmel "to save souls" (Ms A, 69v). She comes back to this desire further on when she emphasizes her theocentric intention (47–47).

9: *degree of glory:* cf. RP, p. 389; TH, pp. 52f. On the connection between love and glory, according to Saint John of the Cross—whom Thérèse is probably recalling here—cf. e.g., *Spiritual Canticle*, st. 38: "What You gave me on that other day."

11–13: *to be a Saint but...helplessness...Yourself my Sanctity:* here we have the essence of the little way: irrepressible desire, awareness of impossibility, new impetus in hope; compare with Ms A, 32r and Ms C, 2v. This insistence on the desire for sanctity (a constant in Thérèse's life, cf. LT 107) is not an egotistical turning in on her own perfection, but the desire to make God "happy" by being "what He wants us to be" (Ms A, 2v). Perhaps

Thérèse also has in mind what she will express in 1896 in regard to "victims": "in times past [they had to be] victims pure and spotless," whereas she knows she is "imperfect" (Ms B, 3v). But she declares here her good will and leaves it to God, the only Holy One and author of our holiness. It is for him then to sanctify his "victim of holocaust."

III. 14–26: "Infinite Merits of Our Lord...Treasures of the Church"
(Ms A, 46r)

Thérèse's offering, however personal it may be ("of myself"), takes place in the church, in this communion of saints that ravished her with "joy and hope" (DE, p. 615). To the Father (subject of lines 14–19) she offers the "only Son" given by him. To the "Blessed Trinity" she offers the saints, the angels, the Virgin Mary (20–26). It is hard not to think here of the song of John of the Cross: "Mine are the heavens...the earth...the just...the angels...the Mother of God...because Christ is mine and all for me.... [My soul], yours is all of this and all is for you" ("Prayer of a Soul Taken with Love"; cf. LT 137 and 182).

14–15: *Since You loved me:* cf. Jn 3:16 (gospel read during the octave of Pentecost) and Pri 13.

16: *my Spouse:* she insists on this (26) probably the better to appropriate his merits; cf. already in LT 129: "these are not our merits, but those of our Spouse which are ours that we offer to our Father." The three mentions of the "Beloved" (27, 52, 66) and the image of "embrace" (64) give a nuptial tone to the offering.

16: *His merits:* Thérèse loves to emphasize the infinite character of Jesus' merits; cf. Ms A, 46r (concerning the Pranzini incident, which she wrote down around the same time as that of the Act of Offering); Pri 7.19; 10.7; 13.15; Ms A, 32r.

18–19: *through the Face of Jesus:* this is quite different from dissimulating behind a borrowed mask. Thérèse often mentions her resemblance (as redeemed) to the Face of the Savior in his Passion (cf. Pri 11). But in 1895, she is enraptured above all by the beauty of the Holy Face (cf. PN 20). Probably this is the transformation to which she aspires here, for the Father's joy. Cf. Saint John of the Cross: "And having looked at them, with his image alone, clothed them in beauty"; and "only with this figure, his Son, did God look at all things," to make them "very good in the Word, his Son," not only did he communicate "natural being and graces" but "a new beauty...supernatural being" (*Canticle*, 3.3–4). In a rather similar sense, Thérèse once wrote: " all creatures become crystal clear when seen through the Face of the most beautiful...of Lilies" (LT 105).

19: *in His Heart burning with Love:* words originally missing from the first draft (sheet A) then added at the request of Sister Marie of the Sacred Heart; cf. p. 84. In fact, Thérèse indeed contemplates the "Heart" of Jesus on June 9: "O my God! Is Your disdained Love going to remain closed up within Your Heart?" (Ms A, 84r). But she does not give it the restricted meaning it could have received at the end of the 19th century. Rather, we should translate it as "bosom" from which overflow "floods of infinite tenderness" (line 58) as in PN 24.10 (a poem whose stanzas 10 and 11 are like a rereading of the offering of June 9; cf. *Poésies*, vol. 2, p. 158).

20: *I offer You:* The beginning of a new paragraph on sheet C (absent from sheet A) makes us think that Thérèse is addressing the whole Trinity now and not just the Father alone.

22–24: *finally...my dear Mother:* we pointed out above the two additions made to sheet A (lines 14–15). Thérèse will justify her bold appropriation of Mary's love and merits in PN 54.5: "The treasures of a mother belong to her child."

24–26: *It is to her I abandon my offering:* She will read the Act at the foot of Mary's statue. This gesture expresses a constant reality in the life of Thérèse who gives everything back to God through Mary's hands.

IV. 26–38: "IMMENSE DESIRES"

After recalling Jesus' promise (28–29), she addresses him now (30–38) slipping imperceptibly from one divine Person to the other. From offering she passes to request in order to make known her "immense desires" (31, originally "infinite"). Relying on Jesus' word and on the authority of Saint John of the Cross (30), she asks "confidently" (31), "certain" (29) of being heard. She does it on a solemn note that heralds something important.

28–29: *Whatsoever...will give:* Jn 16:23. This is the first mention in Thérèse's writings of this promise, which we find again in Pri 13 and Ms C, 35v.

29–31: *desires...to desire...immense desires:* Thérèse relies as much on her own desires as on Jesus' promise, for in them also she sees his work in her.

30: *the more You want to give:* Saint John of the Cross, letter 15, to Leonor de San Gabriel (July 8, 1589): "The more he wants to give, the more he makes us desire." In Thérèse's French edition, Maxim 45 reads: "The more God wants to give us, the more He increases our desires." It is under this form that Céline transcribed it in Thérèse's scriptural notebook, p. 6 (see VT no. 78, April 1980, p. 151). In 1895, the Carmelites of Paris published an offprint of the *Maxims and Spiritual Counsels*. From then on, Thérèse had a copy for her own use; cf. DE, p. 844 and CG II, p. 854. With time, Thérèse's certitude became ever stronger: "He is the one who makes us desire and who grants our desires" (LT 201). Cf. Ms C, 31r; LT 253; CJ 13.7.15 [HLC, p. 94], and note. In the infirmary, it is again this doctrine of St. John of the Cross that will sustain her hope in her mission after death; cf. CJ 16.7.2; 18.7.1 [HLC, pp. 100–102], etc. Thus, Thérèse received from St. John of the Cross one of the great secrets of her prayer.

31: *immense desires:* first version (sheet A) reads "infinite desires." With Mother Agnes, Thérèse will take a mischievous revenge on the "theologian" who in June 1895 asked for the correction; cf. LT 230. She speaks of "infinite desires" as early as LT 107. At Christmas 1894 she had the Child Jesus say: "[souls] I made for myself / I made their desires infinite" (RP 2, 6v). A new illustration of Thérèse's approach: she does not limit God to the measure of human beings (whether it be their sin or their desires) but fits them to God's measure by opening them up to the infinite (cf. Catherine of Siena and Thomas Aquinas).

31–34: *take possession...from your little victim:* this passage should be read at one go. What is Thérèse asking for? She does not have the benefit of daily communion (cf. the regulations regarding this in the *Constitutions* of 1581 and the *Ceremonial* of 1888). The fault lies with the prioress, first with Mother Marie de Gonzague, who could not fall in line with the Decrees of 1891 (cf. PO, 152), then with Mother Agnes of Jesus, at the time of the Offering to Love (who did not dare act freely in this area). On this June 9 could not Thérèse beg for a miracle that would make (her superiors) change their minds, by her prayer alone, without awaiting her death (cf. PO, 249)? She did it in other circumstances; cf. Ms A, 82v. But would daily communion itself have fulfilled her "infinite desires"? Moreover, Thérèse does not receive the Eucharist "for her own consolation" (Ms A, 79v), in a kind of appropriation. To ask that she might take "possession" of the sacred host in a static and permanent way for her own consolation is truly not her style. Besides, it would be a useless miracle which would not exhaust the purpose of the sacrament: transforming nourishment.

In fact, she asks to be taken "possession" of by him who transforms bread into his Body so he may transform the communicant into himself. She desires this transformation, dynamic and wholly sacrificial, to be as real as possible, through the sacrament above all, or without it when it is impossible for her to receive it.

This interpretation alone seems to us to assure the coherence and authenticity of Thérèse's sacramental doctrine: cf. "No doubt it is a great grace to receive the Sacraments; but when God does not permit

it, it is good nonetheless, everything is a grace" (CJ 5.6.4 [HLC, p. 57])
where it is a question of the "last sacraments": communion as Viaticum
and Extreme Unction, whose reception is obligatory for a Carmelite!).

Thérèse knows that God is not a prisoner of the means of salvation he offers us in the church (cf. Ms A, 3r, where he comes to "the
poor savage" even without baptism). In what concerns her, Thérèse will
neglect nothing in order to benefit from the means, and from the Eucharist above all. When ill she will make heroic efforts "to gain one
Communion" (CV 21/26.5.6 in DE II, p. 38) and will seem "ready to die
of sorrow" when she will have to give it up (DE II, pp. 302–304). Having
accepted that, she does not confuse the means with the end. In fact, her
desire for this possession of herself by Jesus even preceded her first communion; cf. LT 11 where she wishes "that the little Jesus be so at home
in my heart He will think no more about going back to heaven." Cf. VT
no. 76, October 1979, pp. 311f.

On this important subject, let us note again that in the first half
of 1895, Thérèse recalls in her manuscript her communions as a child
and as an adolescent (Ms A, 35r, 36r, 48v). She is then led to articulate
her eucharistic doctrine more precisely, while "the attraction she felt to
receive her God" as in "the living temple of the adorable Trinity" (48v)
is rekindled. The inspiration of June 9 brings her, among other things,
the answer to an impossible desire: "It was enough that she ask Him with
confidence to take possession of her. Her soul will then become, in the
strictest sense of the term, a victim, where, as in the Tabernacle, the
transforming presence of the Holy Trinity will be assured" (A. Combes,
*Note sur la signification historique de l'offrande Thérésienne à l'Amour miseri-
cordieux* [Note on the historical meaning of the Theresian offering to
Merciful Love], 1949, offprint, p. 11). However that may be, it is after
the Act of Oblation that Thérèse, playing on the equivalence of host/
victim (cf. line 34, note) reaffirms this truth: "We are also hosts / Which
Jesus wants to change into himself" (PN 40.6).

For all these reasons, we leave to Sister Marie of the Trinity the
responsibility for an interpretation that it does not seem to us we can
follow; cf. VT no. 77, January 1980, CSM no. 39 and notes. After having
followed her in the same line of thought at the Process (PO, 158f.; PA,
161f.), Mother Agnes will retract her statement in private. To others
she will write, for example: "Our Thérèse requested and truly expected
this privilege, and I am sure that she was not disappointed in her expec-
tation as regards the union of her soul with her God, which she wanted
to be so complete. But I never heard her say a single word that would
make us suppose she thought of the perpetual presence of the Sacred
Host within her. I do not know if I am expressing myself well" (Letter to
the Carmel of Avignon, July 22, 1926). One can consult the Center of

Documentation at Lisieux for a complementary dossier on this much debated question.

34: *hostie* [*victim/host*]:"The word host is the equivalent of Victim for her" (Sister Geneviève, *Little Catechism...* p. 30, n. 1). Thérèse found this equivalence in the translations of Wis 3:6, pointed out above in regard to the title (1–3). We find further proof of it in Ms B, 3v; cf. the same PN 29.11–14, where it slips from "victim" to "host"; PN 40.11 (*Poésies*, vol. 2, 234); as well as the interesting testimony of Sister Marie of the Eucharist in VT no. 99, July 1985, pp. 29f., 33–35.

35–38: after the Eucharist comes Penance (without the word), the sacrament that purifies, consumes, and transforms. There again, at each instant Merciful Love can realize fully the specific effect of the sacrament, even if it isn't possible to have recourse to it after every fault committed (in Thérèse's time the Carmelites went to confession every week).

35: *ingratitude of the wicked:* for a heart as grateful as Thérèse's, ingratitude seemed to her "what He (Jesus) must feel the most" (LT 122) because it is a lack of appreciation of His love (cf. RP 2.3r; RP, pp. 87, 309). But it is not just the "wicked" who act thus: cf. Pri 4.9; 15.24; LT 108, 119, 196 (=Ms B, 1v), 246.

35–36: *to take away my freedom to displease You:* compare with the account of her first communion: "Had not Thérèse asked Him to take away her liberty," etc. (Ms A, 35r). Cf. also Ms A, 83v; "through *love*, not through fear, [no one would ever consent] to cause Him any pain" (Ms A, 83v); and the testimony of Sister Marie Philomène: "to avoid all voluntary faults, not because of the pain [i.e., of a punishment to be undergone] but to give pleasure to God" (quoted in VT no. 99, p. 54).

36: *immediately:* cf. "quickly" (Ms A, 83r) and "in an instant" (83v); Sister Marie-Philomène: "He wipes out our involuntary [faults] as soon as we commit them" (*loc. cit.*). It is important not "to make a habit of these continual indiscretions" without going to Jesus to ask pardon as soon as we realize our faults (cf. LT 258). Compare this "immediately" with "in an instant" (54) and "without any delay" (63) with implicit reference to purgatory.

36: *may Your Divine Glance cleanse me:* Thérèse could have read in the *Spiritual Canticle* in many places: "With God, to gaze at is to love" (*Canticle*, 32.3); "God's gaze cleanses [the soul] first of all, then makes it agreeable to him" (cf. *Canticle*, 33.6); "when God looks, he loves and grants favors" (*Canticle*, 19.6). This is far from the severe look of a God irritated with sin.

37–38: *consuming...into itself:* possible reminiscence of the *"Gloss"* of St. John of the Cross or the *Canticle*: "In this wine cellar these herds of imperfections are more easily consumed than are the rust and tarnish of metal consumed by fire" (*Canticle*, 26.19). In Thérèse's scriptural notebook, Céline recopied this Maxim, the end of which we place in italics: "God desires to make gods of us, through participation in what he is himself by nature, just as the fire converts everything into fire." By giving "weakness" and "imperfections" their place, the Act of Oblation is in complete accord with the "little way." In 1896, Thérèse will insist even on the positive advantage of weakness: "Understand that to love Jesus, to be His victim of love, the weaker one is [...] the more suited one is for the workings of this consuming and transforming Love" (LT 197).

V. 39–43: THE CROSS AND THE GLORY

In 1896–1897, Thérèse had to integrate into her offering to Love a painful dimension not foreseen at the outset. On the morning of June 9, 1895, joy alone sustained her. Her gaze always fixed on Jesus (39: "O my God!"), she contemplated him with his stigmata in glory and aspired to perfect transformation (sheet A reads "perfectly"; sheet C did not keep this correction). We cannot go into the problem of "Thérèse and suffering" here (see DE, pp. 485, 500), but it is enlightening to place this paragraph in the context of the year 1895, framed on one hand by Ms A, 3r and PN 16 and 17, and on the other by Ms A, 83r.

39–40: *I thank You...of suffering:* Thanksgiving for all her past life is the whole momentum of all of Ms A. In spring 1895, Thérèse gives thanks "in particular" for this "ineffable grace / Of having suffered" (PN 16.1). She does not ask for it to be renewed nor does she refuse it. The "crucible of suffering" refers probably to Wis 3:5–6 (cf. BT, pp. 117f.).

42: *I hope...sacred stigmata of Your Passion:* rather than Gal 6:7, probably we should think of Jn 20:27 where the resurrected Christ shows his wounds. In 1896, Thérèse will evoke the "Good Shepherd... showing His feet, His hands and His heart adorned with luminous wounds" (LT 190). We know how, at first, Sister Marie of the Sacred Heart had refused to offer herself as a victim of love, for fear of suffering: "Certainly not...God would take me at my word and I have too great a fear of suffering" (cf. CG II, p. 896). Later, many readers of *Story of a Soul* will ask themselves the question that Sister Geneviève tries to answer in her *Little Catechism:* "Does the *Victim of Love*, by virtue of its offering, dedicate itself to exceptional sufferings?" (p. 30). The answer flows from an attentive reading of the paragraph studied above.

VI. 44–54: "Empty Hands"

From the "last day" of the world (41), Thérèse passes to her own last day, the "evening of this life" (48). Saint of the present moment and spiritual poverty, she has no reserve: neither debts to expiate in purgatory (cf. 36–37 and 54) nor merits to show as a right to recompense. Everything is purified or "spent" from day to day; cf. CJ 12.7.3; 14.7.2 [HLC, pp. 91, 96]; CSM no. 7 (VT no. 73, January 1979, pp. 58f.), etc. Thus she distances herself even from Saint Teresa of Avila: "Cost what it may, Lord, do not desire that I come into your presence with hands so empty, since the reward must be given in conformity with one's deeds" (*Life*, 21.5). The preachers Thérèse heard (P. Pichon, P. Lemonnier) spoke no differently. The same is true for the circulars of deceased Carmelites at this period; one sister repeated often that she "had not yet done anything for eternity and that she didn't want to appear before God with empty hands"; another is praised for having "appeared before the throne of God with her hands filled with merits." The sister of Luçon whose circular was read June 8, 1895, repeated while she was dying: "I do not have enough merits; I must acquire them." Thérèse does not deny that she has merits (Ms C, 33r–v; CJ 18.8.3 [HLC, p. 152]), but she refuses to store them up. And above all, here, as in the whole offering, it is a question not of giving but of receiving freely.

44: *enjoy You:* cf. PN 24.9.5: "to enjoy your sweet presence in Heaven"; PN 17.4.5: "In Heaven I'm to live on joy." This "fruition" of God is indeed Thérèse's supreme hope, which is wholly oriented toward happiness.

45: *not to lay up:* contrary to Ms A, 33r or LT 65 and 91 ("to lay up treasures for heaven") or even Pri 4.14.

46: *with the one purpose of pleasing You:* one of the guidelines of spiritual childhood, reconciling generosity and gratuitousness; cf. the concordances. Likewise, CSG, p. 57: "My chief desire through life has been *to give pleasure to the good God.* How sorely tempted to discouragement I should be at present had it been otherwise—if, for instance, I had been intent on storing up merit for myself" (*Memoir*, p. 64). See also CSG, pp. 46, 186, etc.

46: *to console Your Sacred Heart:* Marie of the Sacred Heart added these words on her own copy. Thérèse will write them in on her sheet A.

48: *In the evening of life:* cf. John of the Cross, "Sayings of Light and Love," no. 60, which Thérèse quotes in LT 188: "in the evening of life, they will examine you on love."

49: *to count my works:* cf. CJ 15.5.1; 23.6.1; 6.8.4 [HLC, pp. 43, 67, 137]. Thérèse does not deny having works, but she refuses to rely on them for her confidence on the last day.

49: *our justice...stained:* cf. Is 64.6. This is one of the stereotyped formulas which end a number of Carmelite circulars of that time.

52: *O my Beloved:* It is indeed Jesus whom Thérèse continues to address since line 30; likewise, further on, line 66.

53: *time is nothing:* This is an old certitude of Thérèse; cf. LT 114: "Jesus does not look at time since there is no longer any time in heaven."

VII. 55–76: "I Offer Myself"

55: *an act of perfect Love:* Thérèse's one desire is to actualize her love as perfectly as possible, at each moment. She does not hesitate to propose this demanding ideal to such sisters as Marie-Madeleine (Pri 5, 5r), Martha of Jesus (Pri 7, "a new life of which each moment will be an act of love"), Marie of Saint Joseph (PN 28.2: "And my life is but one act of love"). In the infirmary, she will emphasize the repercussions of her offering even in the simplest acts: "Everything that I do, my actions, my looks, everything, since my Offering, is done through love" (CJ 8.8.2).

56: *consume me incessantly:* this is one of Thérèse's most constant wishes since her earliest days in religious life.

63: *without any delay:* cf. "straightaway" in PN 23.8.8; the whole stanza explicitly refers to "purgatory." Again, Thérèse goes against the current of the Carmelite literature of her time: the great majority of the circulars scarcely consider that the most fervent Carmelite will escape expiation in purgatory. Among many sisters we note the fear of this obligatory passage "through fire" (PN 23.8.2). Among her own sisters of Lisieux, the "little doctrine" of Thérèse on this point met with reserve.

64: *eternal embrace:* cf. Arminjon: "Eternal life... nuptial where the soul will clasp her Creator in an eternal embrace" (quoted in *Poésies,* vol. 2, p. 211). Compare with RP 3, 12v 25–26: There... on the Heavenly shore / He will embrace me forever." Thérèse frequently encountered this nuptial term of "embrace" in the *Spiritual Canticle* in connection with the spiritual marriage of the soul with God.

67–68: *renew this offering:* In the infirmary, Thérèse attests "Very often, when I am able, I repeat my offering to Love" (CJ 29.7.2); she desires to renew it "at each beat of her heart." Cf. Pri 10.5.

69: *the shadows having disappeared:* cf. Song 4:4; sheet A reads "the shadows wane."

71. *Face to Face:* cf. 1 Cor 3:12 (and BT, p. 272).

Prayer 7

[Prayer to Jesus in the Tabernacle]

Jesus +

July 16, 1895

O God hidden in the prison of the tabernacle! I come with joy to you each evening to thank you for the graces you have given me. I ask pardon for the faults I committed to-day, [5]which has just slipped away like a dream....

O Jesus! how happy I would be if I had been faithful, but alas! often in the evening I am sad because I feel I could have corresponded better with your graces.... If I were more united to You, more charitable with my sisters, more humble and more mortified, [10]I would feel less sorrow when I talk with you in prayer. And yet, O my God, very far from becoming discouraged at the sight of my miseries, I come to you with confidence, recalling that "those who are well do not need a doctor but the sick do." I beg you, then, to [15]cure me and to pardon me. I will keep in mind, Lord, "that the soul to whom you have forgiven more should also love you more than the others"!... I offer you every beat of my heart as so many acts of love and reparation and I unite them to your infinite merits. I beg you, O my [20]Divine Bridegroom, to be the Restorer of my soul, to act in me despite my resistance; and lastly, I wish to have no other will but yours. Tomorrow, with the help of your grace, I will begin a new life in which each moment will be an act of love and [25]renunciation.

Thus, after coming each evening to the foot of your

Altar, I will finally reach the last evening of my life. Then will begin for me the unending day of eternity when I will place in your Divine Heart the struggles of [30]exile!

Amen.

DOCUMENT: CE II, 180r–v, copied from the original that was later destroyed, as were Pri 3 and 4.

DATE: July 16, 1895.

COMPOSED FOR: Sister Martha of Jesus, at her request (PA, 590), for her 30th birthday.

PUBLICATION: HA 53, p. 251; long extract in Sister Martha's disposition, PO, 429.

CIRCUMSTANCES: Sister Martha did not leave any information on the reason for her request. Given the content of this prayer, it would seem she asked for a text to help her in her evening examination of conscience. As a lay sister, she was not obliged to recite the canonical Office, in particular, Matins (at 9:00 P.M.) which is followed by an examination of conscience in choir (cf. *Spiritual Direction*, pp. 74–79). Her day ended with a visit to the Blessed Sacrament during the Great Silence (8:00 P.M.). She included in it her examination of conscience, often a rather disagreeable exercise, especially for a temperament that easily inclined to "melancholy" and was prone to "discouragement" (Pri 7 and 20). Thérèse writes this text a few weeks after her offering to Merciful Love. It is also contemporary with *Jesus at Bethany* (RP 4).

NOTES

8–10: *If I were...in prayer:* Strictly speaking, we do not find a method of prayer in Thérèse's writings. Thus, these lines are even more precious. Like the counsels of St. Teresa of Avila in the *Way of Perfection,* they indicate the practical conditions for prayer: union with God throughout the day, mutual charity, and self-denial.

11: *very far from becoming discouraged:* cf. Pri 20: "discouragement is also pride." Since her childhood, the refusal to be discouraged has been a very Theresian attitude; cf. her resolution at her first communion: "I will not become discouraged" (VT no. 74, p. 134); as well as Ms B, 3v; Ms C, 2v, 6v, 17v, 31r; LT 26, 143, 150, 202.

13–14: *Those who are...but the sick:* cf. Mt 9:12.

16–17: *the soul...more than the others:* cf. Lk 7:42–43.

18: *love...reparation:* Along with LT 108, the only mention of the word "reparation." We should not force the text by interpreting it here as reparation by love.

20: *Restorer:* only use of this word. To consider Jesus as the only "Restorer" of humankind stems from the most ancient patristic and monastic traditions. Possibly Thérèse encountered this expression in the *Little Breviary of the Sacred Heart,* one of the rare books for her personal use (cf. DE, p. 843); see this little volume for Friday None. But we cannot be certain about this.

23–24: *a new life:* See Martha's promise to Thérèse in December 1892 "to begin a new life" (Ms C, 21v on a very personal matter), but especially "Merciful Love renews me" (Ms A, 84r) and "Your soul is rejuvenated" (RP 4, st. 4), etc.

24: *an act of love:* cf. Pri 6.

25: *renunciation:* a very rare word in Thérèse's writings (Ms A, 33r and 48r) even though she lived it constantly.

27–28: *the last evening...unending day:* we pass from one to the other without transition, as if there were no question of purgatory (because everything has been restored "each evening" by the "infinite merits" of Jesus and by Martha's "love"). Likewise, we pass from struggle to rest on the "Divine Heart." Compare this ending and several aspects of this prayer with the poem "To the Sacred Heart of Jesus" (PN 23), which is probably from June 1895.

Prayer 8

[Prayer for Abbé Bellière]

J.M.J.T.

O my Jesus! I thank you for having fulfilled one of my greatest desires, that of having a brother, a priest, an apostle...

I feel very unworthy of this favor. And [5]yet, since you grant your little spouse the grace of working specially for the sanctification of a soul destined for the priesthood, I offer you joyfully *all* the *prayers* and [10]*sacrifices* at my disposal. I ask you, o my God: not to look at what I am but what I should be and want to be, a religious wholly inflamed with your love.

[15]You know, Lord, that my only ambition is to make you known and loved. Now my desire will be realized. I can only pray and suffer, but the soul to whom you unite me by the sweet bonds of [1v] [20]charity will go and fight in the plain to win hearts for you, while on the mountain of Carmel I will pray that you give him victory.

Divine Jesus, hear the prayer I offer you [25]for him who wants to be your Missionary. Keep him safe amid the dangers of the world. Make him feel increasingly the nothingness and vanity of passing things and the happiness of being able to despise them for your love. [30]May he carry out his sublime apostolate on those around him. May he be an apostle worthy of your Sacred Heart....

O Mary! gentle Queen of Carmel, it is to you that I entrust the soul of the future [35]priest whose unworthy little sister I am. Teach him even now how lovingly you handled the Divine Child Jesus and wrapped him in swaddling clothes, so that one day he may go up to the Holy Altar and carry in his hands ⁴⁰the King of Heaven.

I ask you also to keep him safe beneath the shadow of your virginal mantle until [2r] the happy day when he leaves this valley of tears and can contemplate your splendor ⁴⁵and enjoy for all eternity the fruits of his glorious apostolate....

Thérèse of the Child Jesus
unworthy Carmelite religious

DOCUMENT: afd 13.1 x 20.4 cm; graph paper, 4 x 4. The addressee signed and dated it after Thérèse. The autograph was returned to Carmel after Abbé Bellière's death. The separate folio sheets have been joined together with cellophane tape (1950–1960).

DRAFT: afs 20.7 x 20.4 cm; blue paper from the Martin lacemaking enterprise. The text is in very black pencil with numerous crossed out words, especially in regard to the style.

DATE: Contrary to what is written in HA, p. 263, n. 1, Thérèse did not date her prayer. She composed it between October 17 and 21, 1895. In fact, it is on Thursday the 17th during the community wash that Mother Agnes read her the letter received from Abbé Bellière, a letter written on the evening of the 15th and mailed on the 16th. Mother Agnes herself answered the seminarian, at the latest on the 22nd, since he thanked her on the 23rd. With her response she sent Thérèse's prayer, which Abbé Bellière dated October 22, 1895 (or the 23rd, a date he scratched out).

COMPOSED FOR: Maurice Bellière, age 21 (born June 10, 1874). He presents himself as "a seminarian from the diocese of Bayeux, in his second year at the seminary of Sommervieu [...] missionary aspirant enrolled in the Seminary of Rue de Bac, in Paris" (October 15, 1895, VT no.66, p. 139).

COPY: CE II, 141r–v, before the letters addressed "To Reverend Père Bellière, Missionary of Africa" (sic).

PUBLICATION: HA 53, pp. 262f. Abridged copy in the *Annals* of January 1963, p. 19.

CIRCUMSTANCES: One month after arrival at the army barracks, the seminarian, aware of his psychological weakness, asked the prioress of the Carmel of Lisieux that a religious devote herself especially to the salvation of his soul and obtain for him fidelity to his vocation as priest and missionary (cf. letter of October 15, 1895). Mother Agnes of Jesus appointed Thérèse as "sister of this future *missionary*" (Ms C, 31v). It is for her one of the most vivid joys of her life (Ms C, 32r). She herself did not write to her new spiritual brother until the end of 1896, during Mother Marie de Gonzague's term as prioress, but she let him know of her feelings and her desires for him by means of this prayer. On this spiritual friendship, thus begun, which will hold "such a great place in [her] life" (cf. Ms C, 33r) we now have authentic texts and in-depth studies. For the texts: see Ms C, 31v–35v; the LT and LC exchanges between Thérèse and Abbé Bellière (cf. CG II, pp. 1437f and 1392); the notebook of poems transcribed for him, especially PN 18A *and remarks* concerning him: CJ 30.7.4; 12.8.2; 4.9.4; 21.9.3 [HLC, pp. 118, 146, 183, 194] and DE, p. 898; all the letters of Father Bellière to Mother Agnes of Jesus and Mother Marie de Gonzague, in VT nos. 66 and 67, April–July 1977. For the studies, see P. Destombes: AL, January 1963; VT nos. 12, 13, 14, October 1963 to April 1964; and Sister Cécile (= DCL) in collaboration with the White Fathers: VT nos. 66–69, April 1977 to January 1978. The numerous acquisitions of this last series complete and sometimes rectify earlier publications.

NOTES

This Pri 8 is thus the first writing addressed by Thérèse to Abbé Bellière. It is first of all a prayer of thanksgiving and offering (actualizing on this point the Act of Oblation of the preceding June): intercession with Jesus for her brother, through Mary, "Queen of Carmel." From this prayer there emerges also a certain program of spiritual life for the seminarian soon to become a soldier.

1: *O my Jesus:* The rough draft reads: "My God."

2: *having fulfilled...desires:* cf. Ms C, 31v, which situates exactly this desire: a "priest brother" who can replace one of her two little brothers who died in infancy, children whom the Martin parents would have so liked to see as missionaries. Jesus will not only "fulfill" but "surpass" Thérèse's desire by giving her a second spiritual brother the following year, P. Roulland (May 1896).

3: *apostle:* twice in this Pri 8, and twice "apostolate"; cf. also LT 220. Thérèse likes this title—at least as much as she does "missionary"—probably because of its more evangelical overtones.

8: *soul destined:* rough draft: "priestly soul." P. Bellière was not ordained a priest until June 29, 1901, at Carthage.

9–10: *all the prayers and sacrifices:* cf. 1.18. The emphasis on "all" corresponds to the seminarian's request: "especially ... exclusively" (VT no. 66, p. 140). After "disposal" the rough draft even adds: "I want my life to be consecrated to him," an addition struck out later.

14: *wholly inflamed with your love:* this is the prayer that Thérèse will ask her brother to say for her. Cf. LT 220.

18: *to pray and suffer:* this is the "work" of the Carmelite (cf. Pri 6); cf. Ms C, 32r; PN 35.2, a poem that is related to the present paragraph; and *Poésies*, vol. 2, pp. 219–222.

25: *your Missionary:* At that time an aspirant of the Foreign Missions in Paris, in December 1896 Abbé Bellière will be removed from their list and accepted by the White Fathers; cf. VT no. 69, pp. 61–65. He will disembark at the novitiate in Algiers on October 1, 1897, the very day after Thérèse's death; cf. VT no. 67; pp. 206, 210.

26: *Keep him:* We think of Jn 17:15; cf. Ms C, 34v and 35r where Thérèse specifically applies this verse to her spiritual brothers.

26: *dangers of the world:* especially those of the barracks; the "marks of an easy life" are not yet effaced for the young man, as he has just written, and he fears to undergo again the assaults of a world that is not quite dead for him (see letter of October 15, 1895).

32: *Your Sacred Heart:* a favorite devotion of Abbé Bellière who to his signature adds proudly: "Honor Guard of the Sacred Heart"; cf. CG II, p. 823.

37–38: *You...wrapped Him in swaddling clothes:* reminiscent of Thérèse Durnerin's prayer, cf. LT 101 and RP 2, 7v.

42: *virginal mantle:* cf. Ms A, 57r. The rough draft added here: "of accompanying him, and to remind you that it is for the glory of your Divine Son that I address this prayer to you" (lines struck out later).

43–44: *valley of tears:* cf. Ps 83[84]:7; and probably, in this Marian ending, an echo of the Salve Regina.

46: *his glorious apostolate:* the rough draft reads "of his labors." To human reasoning P. Bellière's brief apostolate at Nyassaland (1902–1905) will have nothing "glorious" about it (cf. VT no. 68). But the church of Malawi nonetheless reaped the fruit of his "labors."

47: signature: Note the absence of the word "sister."

On receiving it the addressee affixes his own signature: "Maurice Barthelemy-Bellière, enf. de M. et de J. Guard of Honor of the Sacred Heart A. M. 22 [or 23] October 1895." The first name is that of his adoptive mother, sister of his mother who died eight days after the birth of Maurice. The second name is that of the father, still living (died August 10, 1897), of whom Abbé Bellière never speaks to Thérèse (the deceased father of whom he speaks in LC 186 is in reality his uncle Barthelemy). The abbreviations that follow his name mean "child of Mary and Joseph" (cf. CG II, p. 822) and "Missionary Aspirant." Later, he added in pencil, "of Africa." Meditated on by Abbé Bellière in the chapel at Sommervieu, this prayer followed him to Africa and was returned to the Carmel between 1907 and 1910 with Thérèse's other writings.

Prayer 9

Prayer of Céline and Thérèse

I tell you, if two of you agree on earth about anything you ask, it will be done for you by my Father in Heaven. For where two or three are gathered in my name, I am [5]there among them.

St. Matt. ch. XVIII v. 19–20

O my God! we ask that your two lilies never be separated on earth. Together, [10]may they console you for the little love you find in this valley of tears. For all eternity may their corollas shine with the same brilliance and may they shed the same fragrance when they bow before you!...

[15]Céline and Thérèse
Souvenir of Christmas Night, 1895

DOCUMENT: holy card with lace 12.2 x 7.8 cm (Bouasse-Lebel no. 1563, cf. LT 245, CG II, p. 1279). On the front, a Child Jesus picking lilies; under the picture the printed text: "Happy the lily that remains spotless till the hour of the harvest, its whiteness will shine eternally in paradise." Under the two plucked lilies we read "Thérèse" and "Céline" in Sr. Geneviève's hand—after September 30, 1897—(and not in Thérèse's handwriting: rectifying Mss I, p. 21). On the back in the margin of the printed text, Thérèse's text in pencil, somewhat faded. Above, the biblical quotation; below, the prayer: "O my God!" On the left: "Céline and Thérèse"; on the right, the date. On the silk paper that preserves the front and the lace, Sr. Geneviève wrote: "Thérèse gave me this picture and it is she who wrote what is on the back of it."

DATE: Christmas 1895.

COMPOSED FOR: Sister Geneviève.

COPIES: CE II, 113r, at the beginning of the "Writings dedicated to her sister Céline"; and in CMG IV, p. 369, under the heading: "Little notes—Letters." On the note: "(I found in in my alpargata") i.e., in her hemp sandal, Christmas night.

PUBLICATION: LT 1948, p. 305.

CIRCUMSTANCES: Since she received the habit on February 5, 1895, Sister Geneviève hoped to make her profession on February 6, 1896. Thus, she should have presented her request at the conventual Chapter about six weeks before the end of the year of novitiate, or around Christmas 1895. But the office of Superior—whose authorization is required—was vacant, for Canon Deletroëtte died the previous October 8. His successor, Canon Maupas, would not take up his duties before January 26, 1896. Thus the profession risked being delayed. Moreover, the triennium of Mother Agnes of Jesus expired February 20, 1896. Under these conditions would she have time to receive her sister's vows before the elections? All these uncertainties were not inconsiderable for a novice. Sr. Thérèse surely had Sr. Geneviève's confidences and she did not want these preoccupations to overshadow the joy of Christmas. A very simple gesture emphasized that she was present and watching with sisterly affection: a holy card left in the novice's sandal Christmas night, with a few lines that would make Céline's keenly sensitive heart resonate: her spiritual twinship with Thérèse. No, nothing here below can separate them.

NOTES

Together...the same: these words are at the heart of the "Prayer of Céline and Thérèse." They echo the close union between the two sisters since childhood and especially since Christmas 1886, a union reinforced in 1888–1894 in the parlor or through correspondence, and consecrated by Céline's entry in 1894, "under the same roof...in the same Carmel" (Ms A, 82r). But the quotation from Matthew that precedes the prayer gives it its real atmosphere of faith: "where two or three are gathered in my name." It is "in the name of Jesus" that the two sisters share the same Carmelite life. Thérèse will strongly affirm this: she ardently desires "this happiness not by nature but for her [Céline's] soul so she may walk by our way" (cf. CJ 16.7.2). It is by relying on Jesus' promise that she asks for the grace of the same mission on earth (to console Jesus) and identification of "the two lilies" in eternity.

1–5: *I tell you...among them:* Mt 18:19–20; cf. BT, pp. 170f. Thérèse's prayer will repeat two expressions of this quotation ("we ask" and "on earth"), according to her usual practice.

9: *on earth:* recalling the saying of Jesus. This point, however, poses a problem. At the end of 1895, Thérèse does not exclude for herself the possibility of a departure for the Far East: "Perhaps...transplanted to other shores" (Ms A, 84v). Did she consider from this moment (as during winter 1896–1897) that Céline might accompany her? Cf. LT 207 and LC 172a (this last text is found in *Lettres. Une course de géant* [Letters: A Giant's Course], Paris: Cerf, 1977, p. 481). It is difficult to pinpoint exactly what she means by these words on Christmas 1895.

10: *Together:* this is the central adverb of the prayer, summing up the life of the two sisters, especially the last eight years; cf. CG I, p. 223; CG II, p. 1364; Ms A, 47v and Ms C, 8v.

11: *valley of tears:* Ps. 83[84]:7.

12: *their corollas shine:* the text printed on the front of the card reads: "its whiteness will shine eternally."

12–13: *corollas...same brilliance...same fragrance:* we find here the inspiration of the double daisy of Spring 1892 (LT 134). On this word, "same," describing the life of Thérèse and Céline, cf. LT 47, 57, 65, 96, 102, 124, 127, 134, 141, 144, 167; Ms A, 24v, etc.

Thérèse insists on this perfect equality of the two sisters "in heaven." Throughout the year 1895, Sr. Geneviève had the first copy of each of Thérèse's little autobiographical notebooks (which she bound and offered to Mother Agnes on January 21, 1896). She developed an admiration and enthusiasm for them (cf. *Mes Armes,* p. 112). Perhaps some sadness and disquiet are mingled there: such a superiority of gifts, of virtues and thus of merits in Thérèse, will not this create too great a distance between the sisters in paradise? This fear (rather than jealousy) will become a real torment for Sr. Geneviève during the summer of 1897; cf. DE, pp. 593–608, *passim.* Perhaps Thérèse, who is so intuitive, sought to reassure her Céline on this point too?

Prayer 10

[Morning Offering]

My God, I offer you all that I do today for the intentions and the glory of the Sacred Heart of Jesus. I want to
sanctify [5]every beat of my heart, my thoughts and my simplest works by uniting them to his infinite merits. I want to
repair for my faults by casting them into the furnace of his
[10]merciful love.

O my God! I ask you for myself and those dear to
me the grace to fulfil perfectly your holy will and to accept
for [15]love of you the joys and sorrows of this passing life so
that one day we may be reunited in Heaven for all eternity.

Amen.

DOCUMENT: afs 9.1 x 10.4 cm. Copy in the hand of Sister Marie of the Sacred Heart. She wrote below in pencil: "copy of a Prayer composed by
Sr. Thérèse of the Child Jesus for someone in the world."

DATE: no indication on the MSC copy nor in the Process. HA 53, p. 264,
proposes : "1895, 1896, or 1897." In the absence of the autograph, internal critique alone can offer indications: they seem to point to 1895,
especially the second half of that year.

COMPOSED FOR: Madame de Mesmay, as Mother Agnes indicates on the envelope containing the MSC copy: "Prayer our saint composed for a person in the world (Mme. de Mesmay, friend of Sr. Marie of the Sacred
Heart)." Thus HA 53 and Mss I, p. 22, are wrong in proposing Jeanne
La Neele as the recipient of this prayer. Mme. La Neele does not mention it anywhere in the Process of the Writings (cf. PA, 583). It is probably just a coincidence that CE II transcribes the prayer following
Thérèse's letters to Mme. La Neele. Édith de Mesmay (1860–1927) née
de la Porte de Saint Gemme, was Marie Martin's best friend when she
was a boarder at the Visitation of Le Mans. Cf. S. Piat, *Une âme libre, Marie
Martin* [A Free Soul: Marie Martin], pp. 30–32.

Copy: CE II, 26r. Title: "Act of Offering (Composed for a lady in the world)." Below, a note: "Copy made not from the original but from an authentic copy." This authentic copy is probably that of Sister Marie of the Sacred Heart, source of our text.

Publication: NV 1927, pp. 212f.; Title: "Prayer composed for a person in the world"; repeated in HA 49, first quarter, p. 255.

Circumstances: We know nothing of the particulars but we can hold as certain that Marie of the Sacred Heart asked Thérèse for this prayer for her friend Edith. She did the same with her sister's poems: "As I have no gift for composing such beautiful things, I use the talents of others and afterward I share them with my friends..." (cited in *Poésies*, vol. 2, p. 66).

NOTES

The collections of prayers of the period include a good number of formulas for the morning offering in union with the Sacred Heart, beginning with that of the Apostolate of Prayer, an association Thérèse had been affiliated with since October 15, 1885. Marie Martin and Édith de la Porte, pupils at the Visitation, have in common a great devotion to the Sacred Heart. Let us quote the lines Édith writes to her friend when she leaves boarding school in 1873: "Our hearts will always remain united in the Sacred Heart. We will love Him always, won't we, dear little sister, and *I promise* to recite a little prayer for you each day in his honor. [...] Let us suffer for love of the One whom we will always love, and one day He will reunite us forever." Thus, Thérèse slips right into the sentiments of the addressee (who has become the mother of a family). She does this all the more easily since 1895 is for her the great year of the Sacred Heart (cf. *Poésies*, vol. 2, p. 150). Her formulation is no less personal for that and quite obviously shows traces of the Act of Oblation to Merciful Love.

1: *My God:* here it is the Father, as the rest of the paragraph shows.

2: *for the intentions:* a turn of phrase we find again in Ms A, 46r, LT 218, and Ms C, 33v. We must bear in mind that Thérèse distinguishes between prayer "intentions for someone," i.e., in favor of this person (LT 226), and praying "for the intentions" of this person, i.e., with her, by espousing what the other person holds dear to her heart, as is the case here: "the intentions...of the Sacred Heart of Jesus."

9: *furnace:* a rather rare word in Thérèse's writings; cf. PN 17.6; 28.5; LT 196 (= Ms B, 1r); LT 224. She prefers "foyer [hearth]." She uses "furnace" [fournaise] for the benefit of those whose devotion to the Sacred

Heart is along the lines of Paray-le-Monial: Marie of Saint Joseph, Marie of the Sacred Heart, Abbé Bellière.

9–10: *merciful love:* a specifically Theresian touch since the offering of June 9, 1895. The ending of this paragraph thus proposes to Édith purgatory in this life, such as Thérèse conceives it; cf. Ms A, 84v and PN 23.8.

14–15: *to accept for love of You...joys...sorrows:* a new note quite Theresian; cf. LT 191, 2v; Ms B, 4v ("to suffer through love and even to rejoice through love"); see also the program for holiness that "people in the world can imitate," transmitted to Mme. Pottier by Sr. Marie of the Eucharist from Thérèse (DE, p. 717; July 20, 1897).

Pri 11: Thérèse's shortest prayer, carried over her heart
Make me resemble you, Jesus!

Prayer 11

"Make Me Resemble You!"

Make me R. y

Stamp of the
Holy Face of Tours

Jesus!...

(in other words)

Make me Resemble you, Jesus!...

DOCUMENT: Parchment: 7 x 4.2 cm, folded in two. Inside on the left, a picture of the Holy Face of Tours (a gummed stamp, 25 x 19 mm). Text: above the picture. "Make me R. y"; below: "Jesus!" On the envelope in which it was kept, Sr. Geneviève later wrote in pencil: "Parchment that St. Thérèse of the Child Jesus wore with other prayers in a little container pinned on her chest." This "container" is mentioned in Ms A, 79r. At the end of 1895, it contained at least: the formula of her vows, written in 1890, and the "last tear" of Mother Geneviève (Ms A, 78v and CG II, p. 1274). It also contained a case holding two medals (Rue de Bac and St. Benedict) and five "relics" (a stone from the Coliseum, earth from the tomb of St. Cecilia, a relic of Bl. Margaret Mary, hair of Sr. Mary of Saint Peter of Tours, and another relic of Mother Geneviève).

DATE: Perhaps August, 1895 to August 1896? Research on the development
of her handwriting, use of the Holy Face stamp, etc., leaves a large margin of uncertainty. Internal criticism would situate this prayer around
1895–1896.

PUBLICATION: DE, p. 517; *Poésies*, vol. 1, p. 118.

NOTES

Since 1890, the words of Isaiah 53 illumined for Thérèse all her "devotion to the Holy Face"; "or rather," they were "the foundation of all her
piety" (cf. CJ 8.5.9 [HLC p. 135]), and this short invocation is a synthesis
of it. Thérèse often expressed desires that the contemplation of the Holy
Face inspired in her: "I too, have desired to be without beauty, alone in
treading the wine press, unknown to everyone..." (*ibid.*). She sang this in a
poem, "My Heaven on Earth!" (PN 20). She repeated it in her impassioned prayers (Pri 12 and 16). She sums up all that here in an exclamation of love: aspiration to perfect transformation in her Beloved, configu-
ration to Jesus in his Passion. In this we have the timeless and fundamental prayer of "Thérèse of the Holy Face." "Make me resemble You," cf. PN
20.5: "I will resemble You, Jesus," (August 12, 1895); and Pri 16: "Deign to
imprint in me your Divine Likeness" (summer 1896). "To resemble Jesus"
is found in LT 87 ("To be the spouse of Jesus, we must resemble Jesus, and
Jesus is all bloody"), LT 145 and 201; PN 31, r. 2; RP 1, 12v; RP 3, 18v; Pri
3.15; Pri 6.42. We also find "resemblance" in LT 134 but with a different
nuance.

Pri 12: Consecration to the Holy Face (recto)

Consécration à la Sainte Face.

[Handwritten manuscript text — Consecration to the Holy Face]

Pri 12: Consecration to the Holy Face (verso)

Prayer 12

Consecration to the Holy Face

The words in italics were written by Thérèse in red ink.

[r]   *Lord, hide us in the secret of your Face!...*
      Sr. C. Geneviève of St. Th.-Marie *of the Holy Face*
      Sr. L. J. Marie of the Trinity and *⁵of the Holy Face*
      Sr. Marie F. Th. of the Child Jesus *and of the Holy Face*

For a little of this *pure Love* is more beneficial to the church than all these other works put together.... Thus it is ¹⁰of the greatest importance that our souls be exercised much in *Love* so that being consumed quickly we do not linger long here on earth but soon attain to the vision of *Jesus, Face to Face.*

[v]   *Consecration to the Holy Face*

O Adorable Face of Jesus! Since you have deigned to choose our souls to be intimately yours in order to give yourself to them, we come to consecrate them to you.... *O Jesus,* we seem to hear you say to us: "Open ⁵to me my sisters, my beloved brides, for *my Face* is covered with dew and *my hair* with the drops of the night." Our souls understand your language of *love;* we want to dry your *gentle Face* and to console you for the forgetfulness of the wicked. In their eyes you are still as one hidden; they look upon you as an object of contempt.......

[10]*O Face* more beautiful than the lilies and roses of springtime! You are not hidden from our eyes.... The *Tears* that veil your *divine look* seem to us like *precious Diamonds* which we want to collect to buy the souls of our brothers and sisters with their infinite value.

From your *Adorable Mouth* we have heard your *loving complaint.* [15]Since we know that the *thirst* which consumes you is *a thirst for Love,* we would wish to have *an infinite Love to quench your thirst....* *Beloved Bridegroom* of our souls, if we had the *love* of all hearts, all that *love* would be for you.... Well, give us this *love* and come and *quench your thirst* in your little brides...................

[20]*Souls, Lord,* we need *souls.....*above all *the souls of apostles and martyrs* so that through them we might *inflame* all poor sinners *with your Love. O Adorable Face,* we shall gain this grace from you!.. Then, heedless of our exile on the banks of Babylon, we will sing for your *Ears* the [25]sweetest melodies. Since you are the true, the only Homeland of our hearts, we will not sing our songs in an alien land.

O beloved Face of Jesus! As we await the everlasting day when we will contemplate your infinite Glory, our one desire is to charm your *Divine Eyes* by hiding our [30]faces too so that here on earth no one can recognize us... *O Jesus!* Your *Veiled Gaze* is our *Heaven!...*

Signed:

Th. of the Child Jesus and of the Holy Face—M. of the Trinity and of the Holy Face—G. of St. Th. Marie of the Holy Face

DOCUMENT: Cardboard backing 13.1 x 9.1 cm. On the front, four oval medallions (photos, about 35 x 27 mm; above, Holy Face of Tours; on the left, photo of Sister Geneviève; on the right, that of Thérèse; below, Sister Marie of the Trinity. The original photo of Thérèse, VTL no. 29, is replaced today by Céline's oval painting of Thérèse. Thérèse painted thorn branches around the four photos. Texts on the front: above the Holy Face, verse from Ps 31 [30]:21; under each photo, the name of the

Carmelite; under the group of photos, quotations from St. John of the Cross. Text on the back: the Consecration, with autograph signatures of the three Carmelites. On front and back, the text is in black and red calligraphy.

DATE: All the converging indications point to August 6, 1896, Feast of the Transfiguration: the writing and the themes are those of the summer of 1896; the three photos of those signing were taken on the same day and in the same place and pose a little after July 3, 1896; cf. CG II, p. 873, regarding "Thérèse with scroll" (VTL no. 29).

COMPOSED FOR: herself and two of the novices, Sisters Geneviève and Marie of the Trinity.

FIRST VERSION: There is a rough draft of the Consecration alone, afs 9.2 x 13.1 cm graph paper 4 x 4. The written text is very fine, with numerous corrections. Because of important variants that were not retained in the final version, the text is reproduced below. On the back there are traces of painting (sketches for the thorns on the front, burnt sienna paint).

ANOTHER ROUGH DRAFT: The texts of St. John of the Cross (on the front of this Consecration) are transcribed, with variants, on the back of a sketch of pictures 5 and 6, "Souvenir of a short exile" (summer 1896); cf. VT no. 77, January 1980, p. 77.

COPIES: CE II, 177r–v. The texts on the front are not tken up again, but only the prayer on the back with this title: "Consecration to the Holy Face composed by Sister Thérèse of the Child Jesus for the novitiate." Sister Geneviève and Sister Marie of the Trinity sign in their own hand, as on the original. A copy by Sister Marie of the Trinity in her red notebook, CRM, pp. 137ff.

PUBLICATION: HA 98, pp. 206ff., with two variants. The texts on the front are not published except in Mss I, p. 20.

CIRCUMSTANCES: The Transfiguration is one of the main feasts of the Confraternity of the Holy Face, of which M. Martin and his daughters (Marie, Léonie, Céline, and Thérèse) had been members since April 26, 1885. Initially called Marie of the Holy Face (cf. LT 174), Sister Geneviève chose August 6 as her patronal feast. In 1895, she composed 33 notes "of Reparation" that the sisters drew by lot on that day during exposition of the Blessed Sacrament in the Oratory; they kept up this custom for some 60 years more. Sister Marie of the Trinity—originally Marie Agnes of the Holy Face, cf. PN 11 and 12—was equally very drawn to the Holy Face since her childhood. For August 12, 1895, Thérèse composed for her "My Heaven on Earth" (PN 20), a poem to the Holy

Face. In 1896, Thérèse chose the Feast of the Transfiguration to conse-crate herself solemnly to the "Adorable Face of Jesus," along with those companions whom she already invited in 1895 to offer themselves to Merciful Love, as if one consecration prolonged the other. In 1897, she celebrated August 6 in the infirmary, an occasion of important confi-dences on her "devotion to the Holy Face"; cf. CJ 5.8.7; 5.8.9; 6.8.1 [HLC, pp. 134–135], and the notes in DE. Chronologically, this Conse-cration is placed between the poems "To Our Lady of Victories" (PN 35, July 16, 1896) for P. Roulland, and "Jesus Alone" (PN 36, August 15), written for Sister Marie of the Eucharist (who was not invited to the aforementioned Consecration, as the Holy Face of Tours filled her with repugnance). We are some weeks from the writing of Ms B.

SOURCES: The text should be placed in the overall context of Thérèse's writings on this theme. We know already that the Carmelite of Lisieux owes much to the Carmelite of Tours, Mary of Saint Peter: the latter's *Life* and the various manuals, short works, or leaflets of the Confrater-nity of Tours (cf. LT 95). Let us cite only the *Neuvaine en l'honneur de la Sainte Face* [Novena in Honor of the Holy Face] by P. Janvier (Tours, 2nd ed., 1889) and the *Petit bréviaire de la Sainte Face* [Little Breviary of the Holy Face] by Natalie Blanchet (Tours, 2nd ed., 1889) a work kept in the antechoir in Thérèse's time. According to an oral tradition, the "Litanies of the Holy Face" by Sister Mary of Saint Peter were frequently recited in community. The sisters, taking turns, also recited in private the "Prayers of Reparation" composed by the same sister. It is not sur-prising, then, that several expressions would have passed into this Con-secration and Thérèse's other writings (RP 2, for example, or Ms A).

Certain themes of this prayer appear as early as 1889 under the pen of Sister Agnes of Jesus (LC 102), who initiated Thérèse into devo-tion to the Holy Face (cf. Ms A, 71r). In 1890, Sister Agnes also com-posed a "Prayer to the Holy Face" that Thérèse as a novice loved and quoted (this text is published in VT no. 81, January 1981, pp. 63f.). Nev-ertheless, beyond some borrowings indicated in the notes below, Thérèse draws from her own resources, moved by an original inspira-tion and expressed after carefully working out her thought, as the first version shows. Above all, the unexpected illumination given to her text by the quotations from St. John of the Cross was absolutely her own. It offers an indispensable reading key for a deeper understanding of the Consecration.

NOTES

1: *Lord...your Face:* cf. Ps 31 [30]:21; and BT, pp. 73f. This verse is frequently quoted in the Tours materials. We read, for example, in a consecration they propose: "Most sweet Jesus, hide in the secret of your Face all the members of this association." See also below, the ending of the first version.

2–7: Names inscribed below the photos of the three Carmelites. Thérèse recalls there in initials the baptismal names of each one: "C" for sister Geneviève (Céline); "L–J"(Louise Joséphine) for Marie of the Trinity; "Marie F." (Marie Françoise) for herself. This listing is customary for the taking of vows and their annual renewal. Using it here confers on the Consecration a solemn character, which engages each sister's whole Christian being. Let us note that Thérèse was the first Carmelite of Lisieux to bear the "title of nobility" (cf. LT 118) "of the Holy Face" as well as that "of the Child Jesus."

8–9: *little...put together: Spiritual Canticle,* 29.2. Thérèse's copy reads: "is more useful to the church than all other works put together" (p. 400). This is the first time that the quotation appears in her writings. It will be repeated in Ms B, 4v; LT 221 and 245. Therefore, we could read it here as a rendering, into the words of Saint John of the Cross, of the discovery made by Thérèse, in this summer of 1896, of her "vocation in the Heart of the Church...Love" (Ms B, 3v).

9–13: *It is thus...Face to Face: Living Flame,* 1.34. Thérèse modifies the translation she uses: "It is then of the greatest importance that the soul exercise herself greatly in love, in order that the soul, consuming herself rapidly in him, will not linger here below and will soon see her God face to face" (p. 158, passage that Thérèse will mark with a cross in pencil in the infirmary in 1897, cf. DE, p. 493). Let us note that though she does not cite this saying until 1896–1897, she has been living it for some years; cf. CJ 27.7.5 [HLC, p. 113]: "With what longing and what consolation I repeated from the beginning of my religious life these other words of St. John of the Cross: 'It is of the highest importance, etc.' " By inscribing these words under an image of the Holy Face, Thérèse suggests that the contemplation "Face to Face" to which she aspires is that of "Jesus." Cf. LT 96 (CG, p. 505). The juxtaposition of these two quotations is striking, as if the apostolic zeal of lines 8–9, this "pure Love" so "beneficial to the Church," found its full accomplishment only in the "Face to Face" of heaven. The greatest service of the church then, would demand not so much duration "on earth" as intensity, "much," which should "quickly" lead to boundless fruitfulness after death. This is the germ of the great desire of winter 1896–97 (cf. RP 8, sc. 8: "If I cannot work in paradise for the glory of Jesus, I prefer to remain in exile"). And this is the personal message she will want leave to her three Carmelite sisters (LT 245). Thérèse's posthumous fruitfulness would seem to justify this interpretation. However that may be, we have a new example of the way Thérèse incorporates and reinterprets her sources, including her teacher John of the Cross. And we will have to keep these quotations present in our mind for a deeper insight into the Consecration on the reverse side.

BACK

4–6: *Open...night:* cf. Song 5:2 and BT, p. 113. Thérèse could read this verse each day on the wall of the St. Elias cell wing, cf. CG 1, p. 542.

8–9: *in their eyes...contempt:* cf. Is 53:3 and BT, pp. 130f.

10: *O Face, more beautiful...springtime:* Thérèse often praises the "beauty" of the Holy Face; cf. RP 2, and the end of the first version, p. 124. She takes her inspiration here from the Litanies of the Holy Face: "O adorable Face, fresher than the roses of springtime," adding to it "lilies."

11.29: *hidden...hiding:* cf. Is 53:3.

11: *The Tears:* First version: "which sparkle in your veiled eyes," cf. RP 2, 4r p. 310. Note that Thérèse lingers more often on the "tears" (or "weeping") of the Holy Face than on the Blood, which, however, she does not ignore; cf. PN 20.1; 24.24; CG II, p. 1371, etc. Tears are like the blood of the heart and therefore of Love.

12. *Precious diamonds:* cf. LT 134, end, where she sketches a similar image. On human tears as "diamonds," cf. Ms A, 54r–v, 63v, 78v.

13: *the souls of our brothers:* here, probably "the wicked" or "poor sinners." In the *Little Breviary* of N. Blanchet, sinners are often called "our brothers."

14–15: *complaint...thirst:* cf. Jn 19:28, a verse that struck Thérèse: PN 24.25; 31.5; BT pp. 257f.; *Poésies*, vol. 2, p. 165. It is probably during the same period (July–August 1896) that she completes her picture of Christ on the cross (VT no. 77, January 1980, pp. 69f.), on the theme of thirst.

17: *of our souls:* the first version reads: "take, take all our love," an impassioned invitation. But as the love of the three sisters would not be enough to "quench" the thirst of Jesus, they need not only "a thousand hearts" (PN 24.31) but the love of "all hearts" (l.18).

20: *Souls:* most of the literature of Tours proposes an "Exclamation of love" where we read: "Souls! souls! We need souls."

21: *apostles and martyrs:* that is, missionaries; cf. PN 35, title, and Ms B, where Thérèse is carried away by her desires. In the prayer of Th. Durnerin that she knew by heart (LT 94 and LT 101) and that she had been having the novitiate recite each day since March 1896, we read: "Oh! priests! priests filled with fire!" etc.

23–26: *heedless...alien:* cf. Ps 136[137]:1–4 and BT, pp. 90f.

24: *for your Ears:* the first version reads "to please you." On Thérèse's coat of arms the harp is right next to the ear of the Holy Face.

25: *only Homeland:* cf. PN 20.3; RP 6.11r, p. 377. From this point on the first version contains many scratched out attempts; cf. the continuous text below.

29–30: *by hiding... recognize us:* cf. Is 53:3. If it is not the "only desire" of Thérèse, especially in this summer of 1896, it has nevertheless preoccupied her whole Carmelite life with an exceptional intensity; cf. LT 137, 145, 165; Ms A, 71r; RP 4, st. 33, p. 351.

31: Veiled Gaze: cf. *Poésies*, vol. 2, p. 74. — "Our Heaven": for Thérèse there has been no other gaze since Easter 1896, because "dark clouds" (Ms B, 5r) or even "a wall" (Ms C, 7v) conceal from her the image of "the Homeland." Once again she hides her distress with great discretion, behind a cry of love; cf. PN 32, presentation.

33: the three signatures, in red ink in the hand of each sister involved, are on one line. Each of the "consecrees" will live in her own way her assimilation to the Holy Face.

The surprising final phrase of the first version ("We want your beauty to be imprinted in us and to make us invisible to the eye of creatures") makes explicit what it means, for Thérèse, to be "hidden in the Face of Jesus": to be eclipsed in his "beauty," hidden today, tomorrow revealed in glory.

Pri 12—FIRST VERSION

(Words in italics are different from the final text.)

O Adorable Face of Jesus, since you have deigned *to cast on us your glance of Love* and to choose our souls to be intimately yours in order to give yourself to them, we come to consecrate *ourselves* to you. O Jesus, we seem to hear you say to us: "Open to me my sisters, my beloved brides, for my Face is covered with dew and my hair with the drops of the night." Our souls understand your language of love; we want to dry your *adored* face and to console you for the forgetfulness of the wicked. *For them* you are as one hidden; they look upon you as an object of contempt.

O Face *adorable in our eyes, you are* more beautiful than the lilies and roses of springtime...the tears *that sparkle in your veiled eyes* seem to us like *so many* precious diamonds which we want to collect to buy the souls of our brothers and sisters with their infinite value. From your adored mouth we have heard your loving complaint. Since we know that the thirst that consumes you is a thirst for love, *O Jesus,* we would wish to have an infinite love *so as to* quench your thirst. *O* Beloved Bridegroom of our souls, *take, take all our love...* If we *possessed* the love of all hearts, *Jesus,* all that love would be for you. Well, give us this love and come and quench your thirst in your little brides...Souls, Lord, we need souls!...above all the souls of apostles and martyrs so that through them we might *convert* all sinners to Your love... O adorable Face, *we want to give you joy,* heedless of our exile on the banks of Babylon, we will sing *to please you* the sweetest melodies. *Are you not for our hearts the Heavenly Homeland?*

To sing to give you pleasure, is to leave the alien soil. Yes, we have found on a foreign shore the mysterious star which inflaming us with its fire illumines our path. In Heaven we will see you radiant with glory, but here on earth we want your beauty to be imprinted in us and to make us invisible to the eyes of creatures.

Prayer 13

"Eternal Father, Your Only Son"

All that you ask from my Father in my Name, He will give it to you....

Eternal Father, [5]your only Son, the gentle Child Jesus is mine, [10]since you have given him to me. I offer you [15]the infinite merits of his divine Childhood and I [20]ask you in his Name to call to the joys [25]of Heaven a countless host of little children [30]who will follow the Divine Lamb for all eternity.

DOCUMENT: cardboard backing 8.6 x 12.8 cm; black ink. This is the single breviary holy card that contains Prayers 13 and 14 on the front and 15 and 16 on the back. On the front: citrate 49 x 65 mm, framed with a filament, of the Child Jesus of Ittenbach, called "of Messine" (because it was brought by Sister Marie of the Trinity from her Carmel in Paris on Messine Avenue; cf. DE, pp. 465, 486; VTL nos. 41, 42, 43). Above the photo and on each side, the text of Prayer 13; below, the text of Prayer 14; lines 1 and 8 are in Gothic script. On the back: citrate 31 x 44 mm, framed with a filament, of the Holy Face, identical to the citrate of Prayer 12. Above and in the margins, Pri 15; below, Pri 16; lines 1 and 11 are in Gothic script.

DATE: the handwriting—combining erect, slanted, and gothic script—and the setting, seem to be summer of 1896. At this period, Thérèse, using photos taken by Sister Geneviève, made several breviary holy cards, particularly ones with biblical themes (cf. VT no. 77, January 1980). Possibly this one (Pri 13–16) dates from her retreat, September 7–18, 1896, when she had some free time.

COMPOSED FOR: herself. After her death they found these prayers "in her breviary where they served as bookmarks" (HA 98, p. 260). From the fact that Sister Marie of the Trinity had made herself a copy of them and had asked for a less personal ending for Pri 14, it was wrongly deduced

---

that this autograph was made "for Sister Marie of the Trinity" (an error to be corrected in Mss I, p. 20 and in DE, p. 445).

COPIES: CE II, 176r for Pri 13 and 15; CE II, 176v for 14 and 16; and a copy by Marie of the Trinity, as pointed out above.

PUBLICATION: HA 98, p. 260 for 14 and 16; HA 07, p. 305 for 13 and 15; HA 53, pp. 257f.

SOURCES: concerning Prayer 13, we can consult the *Vie de soeur Marie de Saint-Pierre* [Life of Sister Mary of St. Peter], especially pp. 80, 364ff., 400f., 491, etc., and numerous lace-framed holy cards with texts on the subject of the Child Jesus. But again, Thérèse remains personal and we must study Pri 13 and 14 in the light of her writings and words relative to the Child Jesus.

NOTES

1–3: *All that...He will give:* Jn 16:23; cf. BT, p. 253.

4: *Eternal Father:* the term is rare with Thérèse (here and Pri 15). She prefers "Heavenly Father" (LT 107 and 247; Ms C, 34r–v), "Holy Father" (Ms C, 34v), "Merciful Father" (LT 220), and without an adjective 61 times. The invocation "Eternal Father" is probably inspired by the short "Acts," in the form of litanies, of Sister Mary of St. Peter, cf. her *Vie*, pp. 461–489, where the expression is repeated about 180 times.

5–12: *your only Son...given:* probably an allusion to Jn 3:16, as in the Act of Oblation.

23–29: *to call...little children:* Behind this request we find Thérèse's constant concern for the salvation of very young children; see the converging notes in DE, p. 445; *Poésies*, vol. 2, pp. 221 and 251–254; RP, pp. 313 and 374. "To have little children baptized" will be part of her mission after death (CJ 13.7.17 [HLC, p. 95]).

30–33: *will follow...Lamb:* cf. Rev 14:4; and BT, pp. 286f.

Prayer 14

[To the Child Jesus]

I am the Jesus of Thérèse

O Little Child! my only Treasure. I abandon myself to your Divine Whims. I want no other joy than that of making you smile. [5]Imprint in me your childish virtues and graces so that on the day of my birth into Heaven, the angels and saints may recognize your little bride.

Thérèse of the Child Jesus

For the description, date, and other critical information, see Prayer 13.

NOTES

1: *Jesus of Thérèse:* According to tradition, one day St. Teresa of Avila met a "young child" in the cloister who asked who she was. "Teresa of Jesus," she responded, "and who are you?" "Jesus of Teresa," came the reply. (Note that Thérèse is simply the French spelling of Teresa.) This saying, illustrating the anecdote, is on a holy card with lace that Léonie had given her. Thérèse kept it in her breviary (cf. CG II, p. 1088).

2: *O Little Child:* for her coat of arms, in January 1896, Thérèse chose to represent the Child Jesus in his manger (Ms A, 86r). Here, she had before her a Child of about ten (portrait by Ittenbach). With his left index finger he shows his heart and with his right finger he points to heaven, a detail that touched Thérèse who was in the midst of her trial of faith. She adopted it henceforth as her own and kept it with her in the infirmary; cf. CJ 25.7.4 [HLC, p. 109] and DE, p. 465.

3: *I abandon myself...Whims:* implicit reference to the "little ball" (Ms A, 64r) and the "cluster of grapes" (Ms A, 85v). We sense how crucifying these childish "whims" can be. Cf. RP 5, st. 12.

5: *Imprint your graces in me:* probably an echo of the *Spiritual Canticle.* We know (cf. VT no. 77, CSM, no. 31, p. 51) how Thérèse loved these stanzas of the *Spiritual Canticle:*

When you looked at me
Your eyes imprinted your grace in me...
Since you have looked
And left in me grace and beauty...
Let us rejoice, Beloved,
And let us go forth to behold ourselves in your beauty.

(*Spiritual Canticle,* 32, 33, 36)

Once again, let us point out the important place John of the Cross holds in Thérèse's spiritual journey during the summer of 1896. In fact, this is the fourth time that she draws inspiration from his thoughts to design her breviary holy cards: "A Gloss on the Divine" (PN 30, calligraphy on a holy card); LT 188, card with a picture of the saint and his thoughts on the back; "Consecration to the Holy Face" (Prayer 12r) and the present bookmark (echoes of it in Pri 14 and 16).

5: *childish virtues:* as in PN 13.5 or 24.9 ("virtues of childhood," *Poésies,* vol. 2, p. 158). It is not a question of sentimentality but of those "humble virtues" (PN 35.3) that are opposed to the proud virtue shown by Lucifer a little before (RP 7, *The Triumph of Humility*). In the infirmary, Thérèse will sometimes adopt a childish attitude, tone, or gesture (CJ 11.6.1; 10.7.3; 25.8.3; 5.9.1; 29.9.3). With the passage of time, those around her end up preferring these memories in a nearly exclusive fashion, without realizing that Thérèse lived them amid the hard combat of disease and interior darkness. This is what will give rise to a watered-down version of spiritual childhood. In reality, this charming text (Pri 14) plays the same role among the *Prayers* as the "little child" or the "little bird" in the nearly contemporaneous Manuscript B. The vocabulary, then, must not mislead us. These "childish virtues" demand a total abandonment of oneself.

6–7: *birth in Heaven:* the martyrology's *dies natalis* that Thérèse heard read in French translation every evening in the refectory. Here is the only time she speaks in these terms of her own death. Implicitly, the expression excludes the hypothesis of a detour through purgatory (see the same idea in regard to Mother Geneviève, in Ms A, 78v, who Thérèse is convinced went straight to Heaven).

8: The single signature excludes the hypothesis that this prayer was composed "for Sister Marie of the Trinity" (see above). In June 1897, the latter asked Thérèse, who was then in her wheelchair under the chestnut trees, "for an ending...that everyone can say." Thérèse dictated to her: "so...the Angels and the Saints may recognize in me the features so sweet of Your divine Childhood" (CSM no. 55, cited in VT no. 77, p. 66).

Tout ce que vous demanderez à
mon Père en mon Nom
Il vous le donnera.....

Père Éternel, votre Fils unique le Doux Enfant Jésus est à moi puisque vous me l'avez donné. Je vous offre les mérites infinis de sa divine Enfance

et je vous demande en son Nom d'appeler aux joies du Ciel d'innombrable phalanges de petits enfants qui suivront éternellement le Divin Agneau.

Je suis le Jésus de Thérèse.

O Petit Enfant! mon unique Trésor, je m'abandonne à tes Divins Caprices je ne veux pas d'autre joie que celle de te faire sourire. Imprime en moi tes grâces et tes vertus enfantines afin qu'au jour de ma naissance au Ciel, les anges et les saints reconnaissent en ta petite épouse Thérèse de l'Enfant Jésus.

Pri 13 and 14
(on front of holy card in Thérèse's breviary)

« De même que dans un royaume, on se procure
tout ce qu'on désire, avec l'effigie du prince, ainsi
avec la pièce précieuse de ma Sainte Humanité, qui
est mon Adorable Face vous obtiendrez tout ce que vous voudrez »

(N.S. à S.te M.ie de S.t Pierre)

Père Éternel,
puisque vous
m'avez donné
pour héritage
la Face
Adorable de
votre
Divin Fils,
je vous
l'offre
et vous
demande

en échange
de cette
Pièce
infiniment
précieuse,
d'oublier les
ingratitudes
des âmes qui
vous sont
consacrées et de
pardonner aux
pauvres pécheurs.

Je suis le Jésus de Thérèse.

Ô Face Adorable de Jésus seule Beauté qui ravit mon
cœur, daigne imprimer en moi ta Divine Ressem-
blance, afin que tu ne puisses regarder l'âme
de ta petite épouse sans te contempler Toi-Même.
Ô mon Bien-Aimé pour ton amour, j'accepte
de ne pas voir ici-bas, la douceur de ton Regard, de
ne pas sentir l'inexprimable baiser de ta Bouche,
mais je te supplie de m'embraser de ton amour, afin
qu'il me consume rapidement et fasse bientôt paraître devant
toi : Thérèse de la Sainte Face.

Pri 15 and 16
(on back of same holy card in Thérèse's breviary)

Prayer 15

"Eternal Father, Since You Have Given Me"

"Just as in an earthly kingdom one can procure all one desires with money on which the royal image is stamped, so with the precious coin of my Sacred Humanity, which is my Adorable Face, you will obtain all you desire."
[5](Our Lord to Sister Mary of St Peter)

Eternal Father, since you have given me for my inheritance [10]the Adorable Face of your Divine Son, I [15]offer it to you and I ask you, in exchange for this infinitely precious [20]Coin, to forget the ingratitude of [25]souls who are consecrated to you and to pardon poor sinners.

For the description, date, etc., see Prayer 13.

NOTES

1–4: *Just as...you desire:* a simplified version of the interior words heard by Sr. Mary of St. Peter (on October 28, 1845) and quoted in her *Vie*, p. 234. These became the sixth of the "Promises of Our Lord" to those who honor his Holy Face. Sister Geneviève had made it her sixth "Reparation Note," of August 6, 1895.

Prayer 16

[To the Holy Face]

I am the Jesus of Thérèse

O Adorable Face of Jesus, the only Beauty that captivates my heart, deign to imprint in me your Divine Likeness so that you may not behold the soul [5]of your little bride without seeing Yourself in her.

O my Beloved, for love of you, I accept not seeing here below the gentleness of your Look nor feeling the ineffable kiss of your Mouth, but I beg you to inflame me with your love so that [10]it may consume me rapidly and soon bring me into your presence:

Thérése of the Holy Face.

For the description, date, etc., see Pri 13.

NOTES

1: *Jesus of Thérèse:* See Pri 14, note 1. Thérèse boldly appropriates and transposes the saying about the child Jesus. From the anecdote she passes to the mystery of the name by equalizing her two titles: Thérèse of the Child Jesus and of the Holy Face.

3–4: *imprint…Likeness:* this is the third of the "Promises" recalled in Pri 15: "Our Lord promised me to imprint the features of His divine likeness in the souls of those who will honor his most Holy Face" (January 21, 1847) in the *Vie de soeur Marie de Saint-Pierre,* p. 282. Cf. also PN 20.5 and *Poésies,* vol. 2, pp. 135–137.

5: *contemplating Yourself:* cf. RP 5, st. 16: "A Mirror." Again, probably an echo of *Canticle,* 36, 5: "That I be so transformed in Your beauty that we may be alike in beauty, and both behold ourselves in your beauty […]; this, in such a way that each looking at the other may see in the other their own beauty, since both are your beauty alone." And in the same *Canticle,* see the commentary on stanza 12.

7–8: *not seeing...nor feeling:* a basic attitude of faith in Thérèse that is accentuated still more by the trial of Easter 1896. Out of love she accepts being deprived of sensible manifestations of love (look, kiss). As for the "look," it is the open or closed eyes of Jesus that, for her, determine whether it is day or night: a frequent theme from her pen. Cf. LT 144; if Céline saw "the divine glance...night would become brighter than the day." See also the ending of Pri 3.

8: *kiss of Your Mouth:* cf. Song 1:1; BT, pp. 101 and 116.

9: *inflame me:* cf. Pri 8.14. Let us recall that the verb appears for the first time in RP 2 (p. 96) precisely in regard to the Holy Face. It is the portrayal of Jesus which arouses in her the most ardent love.

10: *soon:* probably an allusion to her dream on May 10, 1896 (cf. Ms B, 2r).

CONCLUSION (Pri 13 to 16)

For analytical reasons, we have treated separately the four Prayers (13 to 16) that Thérèse grouped on a single breviary card. For her, this document is a type of identity card, summing up her religious name. She has a very strong sense of its meaning as completing and defining her baptismal name. "Your name is your mission," she writes as far back as 1890 (LT 109).

In her "Letter of Invitation" to her wedding nuptials (LT 118 and Ms A, 77v) she already displayed her "titles of nobility: of the Child Jesus and of the Holy Face." She saw in them the "dowry" of her Bridegroom. Here, in Prayers 13 and 15, she goes back to the source of every gift, the Father. From him comes "her inheritance" (Pri 15.9) to use and, by that very fact, her "mission." She emphasizes it in the deliberate symmetry of Pri 13 and 15: to the Eternal Father who "has given" her His Son, Thérèse "offers" this same Son in return and, relying on a promise of Jesus, she "asks for" the salvation of her brothers and sisters, "in His Name" or "in exchange." Then, she turns to the "Jesus of Thérèse" who gives Himself to her as *Child* and as *adorable Face.* She offers herself and abandons herself in return. The charming inversion of names (Thérèse of Jesus / Jesus of Thérèse) in reality contains an exacting demand: total reciprocity (Pri 14.1 and 8; Pri 16.1 and 11), including the perfect "Likeness" received as a seal: "deign to imprint" (16.3), "Imprint in me" (14.5). This is the total transformation of love so often invoked by St. John of the Cross. It is a question of becoming "Yourself": "mystery of exchange of identity" (B. Bro).

Prayer 17

"Lord God of Hosts"

Prayer inspired by an image of St. Joan of Arc.

Lord, God of hosts, in the Gospel you told us: "I have not come to bring peace but the sword." Arm me for battle; I burn to fight for your glory but I beg you to strengthen my [5]courage.... Then with Holy King David I can exclaim: "You alone are my sword, You, Lord train my hands for war..."

O my Beloved! I know what combat you have in mind for me; the contest will not be on the field of [10]battle........

I am a prisoner of your Love. I have freely forged the chain that binds me to You and separates me forever from that world which you have cursed.... My sword is nothing but Love—with it I will chase the foreigner from [15]the kingdom. I will have you proclaimed King in the souls who refuse to submit to your Divine Power.

Doubtless, Lord, you do not need such a feeble instrument as myself, but Joan, your chaste and courageous bride, said: "We must [20]fight so that God may give the victory." O my Jesus, I will fight then, for your Love, until the evening of my life. As you did not wish to rest on earth, I want to follow your example. I hope this promise that fell from your [25]Divine lips will find fulfillment in me: "If anyone follow Me, where I am, there also will my servant be. Whoever serves me, my Father will honor."

To be with you, to be in you is my one desire.... This assurance that you give me of its [30]fulfillment helps me to bear my exile while awaiting the glorious day of the eternal Face to Face!...

DOCUMENT: CE II, 175r–v. We do not know when or why the original disappeared from the Carmel archives. It seems that in 1910, for the Process of the Writings, the copyist, Sr. Marie of the Child Jesus, had the original in her hand. The stamp and the mention "Ita est" of Canon Deslandes would be proof of it. The copyist respects the alternation of upright and slanted writings, and certain capital letters characteristic of Thérèse ("Divine lips," for example). But the title and the date in red ink cannot have belonged to the original: "Prayer inspired by a picture representing the Venerable Joan of Arc, composed by the Servant of God: Thérèse of the Child Jesus and the Holy Face." Date: "1895."

DATE: in absence of the autograph, only internal criticism enables us to determine the date. We must first of all eliminate 1895, which CE II proposes, probably based on the date of the photo of Thérèse as Joan of Arc (January 1895) that "inspired" the text. The vocabulary of this Pri 17 is not at all like that of 1895, nor is the overall style. The warlike attitude asserted here appears in the summer of 1896, with RP 7 and Ms B ("I feel the vocation of the warrior"). Nevertheless, it is but one element among others: priest, missionary, martyr, soldier, etc. This is the great flowering of multiform desires. Thérèse was content, then, if we may say, to love for those who fight; cf. PN 35 and Ms B.

It is during the winter of 1896–1897 that her personal commitment in the struggle becomes more pronounced. It finds its culminating expression in "My Weapons" (PN 48, March 25, 1897), a poem to which Pri 17 is related by its vocabulary, its tense style and its rapid tempo. Here it is no longer question of imagery but a truly personal struggle. Evoking Joan of Arc is only a pretext, or better, an example and support on the threshold of the decisive offensive. Thus, we propose the winter of 1896–97 as the date.

COMPOSED FOR: herself. The Process places this prayer at the head of the six composed by and for Thérèse herself (cf. PA, 600).

COPY: an autograph copy probably was sent in March–April 1897 to the Museum of Orléans. At this time, the Carmel of Lisieux sent it retouched photos of Thérèse as Joan of Arc (VTL nos. 11–15). The curator, Mgr Desnoyers, thanks them for these on March 10 and April 7, 1897. On the envelope, Sister Geneviève noted: "With these photographs they have at Orléans a long autograph of Sr. Thérèse of the Child Jesus, copied on the back." A rather vague oral tradition suggests that it would be this prayer, recopied by Thérèse; cf. VT no. 77, p. 71, n. 7. There is no way to verify this hypothesis, as the Museum of Orléans burned down in June 1940.

108   *Prayers of Thérèse of Lisieux*

PUBLICATION: HA 07, pp. 306f., with some revisions and omissions (a new proof that in 1907 the autograph was still at Carmel); *Mes Armes*, p. 120. The NV 1927, pp. 210–212, gives as title: "Prayer to obtain courage in the struggle."

CIRCUMSTANCES: We note first that the prayer is addressed to Jesus, not to Joan of Arc. It is not timeless or impersonal, but a very committed prayer with autobiographical import, well situated in Thérèse's spiritual journey. In this winter of 1896–1897, the tuberculosis was progressing and sapping her strength (DE, pp. 30–31; CG II, pp. 918f.). Thérèse knew her death was imminent. She summoned up her strength. Moreover, temptations against the faith were harassing her, the Enemy was provoking her to a duel. In this solitary combat, she looked to Joan of Arc. It was not the first time; as far back as her childhood, this heroine had been her inspiration (cf. RP, pp. 53ff). In the spring of 1895, Joan's martyrdom by fire, which Thérèse mimed (RP 3) helped lead her to her holocaust of love (Pri 6). From May to July 1897, the reference to Joan enabled her to shed light on the "betrayal" Leo Taxil inflicted on her (PN 50), the meaning of her own premature death (CJ 5.6.2), and the object and extent of her mission after death (RP, p. 327). Here it is her own struggle (of faith, even though the vocabulary doesn't mention it) that she "understands" in the light of Joan's struggle.

NOTES

Destined for "the fight," Thérèse knows she is weak and sends an urgent call for help: "I beg you, strengthen my courage." Weak but determined (the two "buts" of lines 4 and 18), her combat of faith is a combat of love (3 times), for love, with the weapon of love. Above all, she must not let herself be separated from Jesus her "Beloved"; cf. Ms C, 7r: "when my enemies come to provoke me...I run to my Jesus." "To be with," "to be in" him, that alone matters, today in battle, tomorrow in the "Face to Face." And that alone assures the apostolic dimension of a solitary and unknown battle: to "have [Jesus] proclaimed King in souls."

Relying on the Word of God (three quotations and allusions), Thérèse throws herself into the struggle. She does it in absolute hope ("I hope...promise...assurance...fulfillment") and presents herself as "bride" but a "Bride...terrible as an army in battle array" (epigraph of PN 48). She appears as such to us at the beginning of 1897. There will be no more "rest" for her until September 30, 1897 when she will die "weapons in hand" (PN 48.5).

Title: to what "picture" of Joan of Arc does the Process refer? The words "prisoner" and "chain" (in the prayer) would make us think that it refers to VTL no. 13, Joan (= Thérèse) in prison.

(N.B. the following numbers refer to the lines of CE II.)

1: *Lord, God of hosts:* cf. 3 Kgs 19:10,14; BT, pp. 60; *Mes Armes,* p. 108.

2: *the sword:* Mt 10:34; BT, pp. 164f.

4–5: *strengthen my courage:* perhaps Thérèse thinks of Judith (Jdt 13:7); BT, pp. 64ff. Cf. also PN 49.4.

6: *You alone...to war:* Ps 143[144]:1–2; BT, pp. 92f.

9–10: *field of battle:* cf. Ms B, 2v and LT 224. Used 13 times in her writings, the word "battle" recurs especially in 1896–1897 (9 times).

11: *prisoner...freely:* Thérèse thinks of her free choice of Carmel, a cloistered order (cf. Ms A, 58r, 67r, 81v, LT 106 and 201; PN 18.32) and the "sweet chain" of religious vows (PN 10.1; 27.3).

13: *world...cursed:* unique expression from Thérèse's pen. It is the world in the Johannine sense, this world of which Satan, the "cursed Serpent" (RP 7, 4v) calls himself prince. HA 07, p. 306, did not retain this harsh ending.

13–14: *My sword...Love:* cf. LT 183 ("to wield the sword of Love"). On the subject of the different weapons of Thérèse, cf. *Mes Armes,* pp. 121f.

15: *King in souls:* same idea in LT 224, where Thérèse gives an explicit transposition of Joan's mission ("to have a mortal king crowned").

17: *weak instrument:* see 1 Cor 1:27; BT, pp. 266f.; RP, p. 327.

25–27: *If anyone...in honor:* cf. Jn 12:26.

31: *Eternal Face to Face:* cf. 1 Cor 13:12; BT, pp. 271f.; and the ending of the Act of Oblation.

Prayer 18

"O Holy Innocents, O Saint Sebastian"

[r]   O Holy Innocents! may my Palm and my Crown re-semble yours!

O Saint Sebastian! obtain for me your love and your courage so that like you, I may be able⁵to fight for the glory of God!...

[v]   O Glorious Soldier of Christ! you fought victoriously for the honor of the God of hosts and received the palm and ⁵crown of Martyrdom. Listen to my secret: "Like the angelic Tarcisius I carry the Lord." I am only a child and yet I must fight each day to preserve the ¹⁰priceless Trea-sure that is hidden in my soul.............. Often I must red-den the arena of combat with my heart's blood....

O Mighty Warrior! be my ¹⁵protector, sustain me by your victorious arm and I will not fear my powerful en-emies. With your help I will fight until the evening of life, then you will ²⁰present me to Jesus and from his hand I will receive the palm that you will have helped me to win!...

Document: lace-edged holy card 11.9 x 8.2 cm: "The first martyr of the Blessed Sacrament" (Boumard and Son, pl. 593). In a notebook, Sister Geneviève comments: "holy card representing a soldier (for us, St. Sebastian) bringing help to Tarcisius, and two little Angels presenting the palm and the crown" (CMG IV, p. 372). Thérèse lightly colored the persons in red and gold. She accentuated Tarcisius's wound in the fore-head and made the blood flow to the ground, a detail absent from the original lithograph. She mounted the card in a gray support, in Canson style, which covered the text on the back and the margins on the front, allowing to be seen only a ciborium with a radiant host above and these two verses under the picture: "To this valiant soldier whose heart he knows / the Child tells his secret: 'I carry the Lord.' "

The text of Thérèse's prayer is done in calligraphy on the gray paper as follows: on the front, above the picture, invocation to the Holy Innocents; under the picture, an invocation to St. Sebastian; on the back, the prayer: "O Glorious Soldier," framed with a filament.

The creation and the setting of this prayer offer many analogies with those of the "farewell mementos" Thérèse left her three sisters; cf. LT 245, described in CG II, p. 1279.

DATE: winter 1896–1897? The feast of St. Sebastian is January 20. The copy of the Process transcribes this text between LT 185 and 211, that is, between March 17 and Christmas 1896. But this fact does not constitute a chronological argument. The application of calligraphy makes an expert appraisal of the writing difficult, as for LT 245. For this last document, the choice of texts indicates someone assured of her approaching death (thus, first half of 1897?). The vocabulary of Prayer 18 has the same tone as that of Prayer 17, whose relationship with "My Weapons" (March 25, 1897) we have already discussed. For these various reasons we propose the beginning of 1897 as the date.

COMPOSED FOR: Sister Geneviève, who will complete one year of profession on February 24, 1897.

COPIES: CE II, 119v, with this title: "Prayer on the subject of a picture representing St. Sebastian and the Holy Innocents (composed for her sister)" and CMG IV, pp. 372f.

PUBLICATION: NV 1927, pp. 213f.; HA 53, pp. 258f. for the whole card.

CIRCUMSTANCES: Prayer 17 was that of Thérèse in the midst of a combat of faith. This is the prayer of Sr. Geneviève in her combat as a young Carmelite, at a difficult moment in the novitiate. But we cannot specify the circumstances further. The recourse to the "Glorious Soldier" is in harmony with Céline's chivalrous tastes (cf. *Mes Armes,* pp. 112–118) and her particular devotion for St. Sebastian. The evocation of the Holy Innocents—children saved gratuitously—suggests a reference to the way of spiritual childhood that Thérèse tried to inculcate in her sister, especially at this time.

NOTES

The vocabulary and the themes are quite Theresian, and are characteristic of this period (beginning of 1897). According to her custom, Thérèse comments and transposes every detail of the picture she is offering her sister: the soldier is identified with Sebastian, cherubs become "The Holy Innocents and who present "the palm" (three times) and the "crown" (twice) to Tarcisius. In the background of the engraving, the Coliseum becomes the "combat arena." In addition, Thérèse takes up word for word expressions from the printed text: "valor... child...secret...I carry the Lord." The continuation of the poem (covered by the gray paper) offers the following alexandrine verses: "Like Tarcisius, you carry the Lord./ Hell will unleash its jealous fury / to ravish the treasure of your happy childhood... / Keep your faith; fight under his victorious banner," etc. The antithesis child / warrior, dear to Thérèse (Ms B, PN 36, LT 194, etc.), suggested by the print is reinforced by invoking the Holy Innocents.

FRONT:

1: Holy Innocents: on this theme, cf. RP 2, 2r; RP 6, 5r and 9r; LT 182 where Céline "wants to be like them and not to win a crown"; PN 44.

1–2: Palm...Crown: attributes of the "martyr," cf. Rv 7:9. These are "values" for Sister Geneviève, and they hold a great place in LT 182 and 183.

3: Saint Sebastian: this very popular saint is one of the heroes of *Fabiola,* a much read work at Les Buissonnets (cf. VT no. 71, pp. 238f.). Since 1893, Mother Agnes compared Céline to Sebastian (CG II, p. 700). La Musse, where M. Martin died in 1894, is situated on the plateau of Saint-Sebastien-de-Morsent (CG II, p. 1204). Thérèse included this warrior in the cortège of honor for Céline's Profession (LT 182). Even on her deathbed, Sister Geneviève will still sing: "O great Saint Sebastian, to whom God can refuse nothing!" (January 20, 1959).

BACK:

2–3: God of hosts: 1 Kgs 19: 10, 14 (cf. Pri 17).

12–13: heart's blood: cf. LT 182; PN 54, 23. We have pointed out that Thérèse painted more "blood" on the print than was on the original. All the present phrase has an autobiographical import: Thérèse also fought "to the point of blood" against temptation; cf. Pri 19.

13: arena: Thérèse and Céline saw the Coliseum in November 1887 and this was an eloquent memory for them; cf. Ms A, 60v as well as PN 48 (this word twice).

Prayer 19

[Act of Faith]

My God, with the help of your grace I am ready to shed all my blood to affirm my faith.

(*Another reading*: for each article of the Creed.)

DOCUMENT: an unevenly torn fragment (afs about 2 x 9 cm) from the margin of a letter. The text in light pencil contains poorly formed words. We read first: "With the help of your grace I am ready (written over *voudes?*) O My God, to shed all my blood for each of the articles of the creed (*synpole* [sic]). A variant suggests, after "for," "to" affirm my faith." But the crossed out "O," the "M" covering an "m," the vertical stroke after "God," suggest the following reading, according to Thérèse's conventions: "My God, with the help of your grace, I am ready to shed all my blood for each of the articles of the Creed" (or "to affirm my faith").

DATE: according to the writing and content, we suggest June–July (?) 1897.

PUBLICATION: TH, p. 114.

CIRCUMSTANCES: Since Easter 1896, Thérèse's faith in eternal life had been put to a cruel test. During the retreat of October 1896, she opened her heart to P. Godefroid Madelaine, who advised her to write down the Creed and to wear it over her heart. She then transcribed the Apostle's Creed with her blood and attached it to the end of her gospel.

In 1897 the darkness became more dense, especially after April 19, 1897, the day Leo Taxil revealed his hoax (cf. RP 7). On June 9, 1897, she wrote, "I believe I have made more acts of faith in this past year than all through my whole life. At each new occasion of combat [...] I run to my Jesus, I tell Him I am ready to shed my blood to the last drop to profess my faith in the existence of Heaven" (Ms C, 7r). Probably, it is on one of these occasions that she jotted down on a scrap of paper this "act of faith."

In the infirmary she returned to this subject and revealed to Mother Agnes the prayer she was very careful not to make: "If I said to myself: 'O my God, You know very well I love you too much to dwell on one single thought against the faith,' my temptations would become more violent and I would most certainly succumb to them (CJ 7.8.4 [HLC p. 140] and TH, p. 116.) In this light, the words "with the help of your grace" receive their full meaning. Thérèse confided another time in Mother Agnes regarding these dark thoughts: "I forcefully endured them but while enduring them I do not cease to make acts of faith" (DE, 526). Mother Agnes revealed to Sister Louise of Jesus (a Carmelite of Lisieux from 1919 to 1982) that sometimes Thérèse felt assailed so violently by a spirit of blasphemy that she vigorously bit her lips so as not to utter impious words that came to her in spite of herself (oral tradition, DCL). Thus we can speak of an indirect confidence regarding Prayer 18: "Often I must redden the arena of combat with my heart's blood."

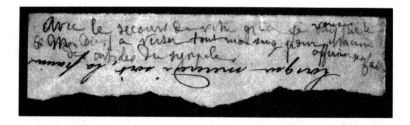

Pri 19
My God, with the help of your grace I am ready
to shed all my blood to affirm my faith.

Prayer 20

Prayer for Acquiring Humility

Jesus!

July 16, 1897.

O Jesus! when you were a Pilgrim on earth, you said: "Learn of Me for I am gentle and humble of heart and you will find rest for your souls." O Mighty Monarch of Heaven, yes, my soul finds rest in seeing you, clothed in the form and nature [5]of a slave, humbling yourself to wash the feet of your apostles. I recall your words that teach me how to practice humility: "I have given you an example so that you may do what I have done. The disciple is not greater than the Master.... If you understand this, happy are you if you put them into practice." Lord, [10]I do understand these words that came from your gentle and humble Heart and I want to practice them with the help of your grace.

I want truly to humble myself and to submit my will to that of my sisters. I do not wish to contradict them nor seek to see whether or not they have the right to command me. [15]O my Beloved, no one had this right over you and yet you obeyed not only the Blessed Virgin and St. Joseph but even your executioners. Now in the Sacred Host I see you at the height of your annihilations. How humble you are, O divine King of Glory, to subject yourself to all your [20]priests without making any distinction between those who love you and those who are, alas! lukewarm or cold in your service... At their word you come down from heaven. Whether they advance or delay the hour of the Holy Sacrifice, you are always ready.......

O my Beloved, how gentle and humble of heart [25]You seem under the veil of the white Host! To teach me humility you cannot humble yourself further. Therefore, to respond to your love, I desire that my sisters always put me in the lowest place and I want to convince myself that this place is indeed mine.

[30]I beg you, my Divine Jesus, to send me a humiliation whenever I try to set myself above others.

I know, o my God, that you humble the proud soul but to the one who humbles herself you give an eternity of glory. So [35]I want to put myself in the last rank and to share your humiliations so as "to have a share with you" in the kingdom of Heaven.

But, you know my weakness, Lord. Every morning I make a resolution to practice humility and [40]in the evening I recognize that I have committed again many faults of pride. At this I am tempted to become discouraged but I know that discouragement is also pride. Therefore, O my God, I want to base my hope in *You alone.* Since you can do everything, deign to bring to birth in my soul [45]the virtue I desire. To obtain this grace of your infinite mercy I will very often repeat: "O Jesus, gentle and humble of heart, make my heart like yours!"

DOCUMENT: CE II, 181v and 183r (182r–v is taken up with notes LT 265, 80, and 119). Destroyed after 1916, the autograph was probably written in pencil.

DATE: July 16, 1897, confirmed by LT 256.

COMPOSED FOR: Sister Martha of Jesus, for her 32nd birthday. We do not know if Thérèse or Martha chose the prayer's theme.

PUBLICATION: HA 07, pp. 307f., with omissions and revisions.

CIRCUMSTANCES: They brought Thérèse down to the infirmary on July 8. She no longer communicated with Sister Martha except through short notes (LT 241, 251, and 256). Sister Martha affirms that she "loves Jesus very much" (LT 251). But her position as a lay sister puts her under the command of any sister and her spirit of contradiction makes obedience difficult for her. Thus Thérèse invites Martha to look at "Jesus gentle and humble of heart," a look that "will bring to birth humility in her heart." At the same period, Thérèse uses identical language with the novices Marie of the Trinity (LT 264), Marie of the Eucharist (DE, p. 778), and above all, Sister Geneviève: "real sanctity is to humble oneself, to bear with one's imperfections in peace...let us run to the last place" (LT 243). It is her own spiritual experience of the moment that Thérèse shares here with Sister Martha: she herself, without giving up the fight (cf. Pri 17, 18, 19), succumbs in sweetness, letting herself be swept away into the "kenosis" of Christ.

NOTES

Thérèse contemplates a "Monarch" made "slave" in the washing of the feet, a Lord obeying "even his executioners": in short, a "King of Glory" who reaches "the height of his annihilations in the Host," at the very heart of his condition as Risen Lord. Such is the "Beloved" whom she wants to join and to imitate, while drawing Sister Martha with her along the same way. In all likelihood the heading "Jesus," the date, and the title are authentic.

1: *Pilgrim on earth:* cf. RP 6, 10v; LT 216 and Ms C, 34r. Thérèse is all the more sensitive to this aspect of Christ's life as the end of her own "long pilgrimage" approaches (cf. LT 263).

2, 10–11, 25, 47: *gentle and humble of heart:* Mt 11:29. These words give Thérèse life. There lies the secret of the "inalterable peace" that she radiates in her last weeks: "I listen with delight to these words of Jesus that tell me all I must do: 'Learn of Me for I am meek and humble of heart'; then I'm at peace, according to his sweet promise" (CJ 15.5.3 [HLC, p. 44]).

3: *Monarch:* a rare word in Thérèse's writings (Ms A, 21v; C, 20r; PN 4.6, RP 3, 6v; RP 6, 7r). Applied to Jesus, it emphasizes—by antithesis with "slave"—his humility; cf. *Poésies*, vol. 2, pp. 237 and 312.

4–5, 18: *clothed...slave...annihilations:* Phil 2:7 (and BT, p. 277).

5, 12, 26, 33: *to humble, humbling:* a quite Theresian word (cf. Index to RP, p. 428).

5: *to wash the feet:* Jn 13:5.

7–9: *I have given you...to practice:* Jn 13:15–17.

10: *I do understand:* a very important word in the Theresian vocabulary (369 times in her writings) and in her spiritual journey. Every new "understanding" Thérèse translates immediately into "practice," all knowledge is turned into love in acts. For the *Prayers*, cf. Pri 2.13; 12v, 6 and 15; Pri 17.8; and twice here.

14: *the right to command me:* this is an important distinction in the daily life of community! Thérèse, for her part, has chosen, especially in these last months, "to obey everybody, in a spirit of faith" (CSG, p. 118; *Memoir,* p. 154). She will tell Sister Geneviève: "You cannot believe you possess [humility of heart] until you are willing to let everybody order you about" (cf. CSG, p. 18; *Memoir,* pp. 18-19).

15–16: *you obeyed:* cf. Lk 2:51.

18: *annihilations:* only use of this word in her writings.

19: *King of Glory:* Ps 23[24]:7, 9; cf. BT, p. 72.

22: *You come down from heaven:* habitual expression with Thérèse; cf. Ms A, 48v, 62v; Ms B, 2v; LT 189; RP 2, 7v; Pri 8.39. But, and this prayer confirms it, Thérèse thinks rather of the abasement, the condescension of Jesus than of a spatial descent.

28, 35: *Last place...last rank:* cf. Lk 14:10, and BT, p. 218

31–34: *set myself above...glory:* cf. Lk 14:11.

36: *share with You:* cf. Jn 13:8.

38: *my weakness...You know:* cf. Ms C, 12v: "You know better than I do my weakness"; LT 247: "never to depend on my strength which is only weakness." This is the Theresian theme par excellence.

43: *hope in You alone:* cf. *Imitation of Christ,* 3, chap. 8, "Those who tell themselves...I am nothing but weakness...place their hope in Jesus alone." This Prayer 20 and the chapter of the *Imitation* are in harmony with each other. Thérèse also refers to it in LT 243.

46: *very often:* same advice to Sister Marie of the Trinity: "To help you, repeat confidently this prayer, particularly at the time of struggle: Jesus, gentle and humble of heart, make my heart like yours. Right away you will feel peace and strength to practice humility" (CRM 86a, in VT no. 75, July 1979, p. 228.)

For a deeper understanding of this prayer, see the dossier on humility (TH, pp. 123ff.); *Mes Armes,* pp. 103f.; and the Process on the humility of the Servant of God. We know the predominant place humility held with Saint Teresa of Avila, whose faithful disciple Thérèse is.

Prayer 21

"If I Were Queen of Heaven"

O Mary, if I were Queen of Heaven and you were
Thérèse, I would want to be Thérèse so that you might be
Queen of [5]Heaven!!!...............
September 8, 1897.

DOCUMENT: Text in violet ink, very shaky handwriting, on the back a card-
board support 6.3 x 9.5 cm (kept in a reliquary) that bears the image of
Our Lady of Victories with the little white flower of May 29, 1887 (cf. Ms
A, 50v).

DATE: September 8, 1897.

COPY: CE II, 112v, following the notes to Sister Geneviève.

PUBLICATION: *Letters* 1948, pp. 438–439, with reproduction in facsimile. The
plate of HA 07, pp. 48f., presents as a "facsimile" of Thérèse this revised
version: O Mary, if I were Queen of Heaven and you were Thérèse, I
would want to be Thérèse to see you Queen of Heaven!"

CIRCUMSTANCES: September 8, 1897, seventh anniversary of her profession,
was a day of peace and sweetness for the ill Thérèse; see CJ 8.9 (DE, pp.
359 and 554f.). She asked to see again the picture of Our Lady of Victories to which she had pinned a little flower that her father gave her when
he gave permission for her to enter Carmel (Sister Geneviève, PO 309).
It is then that she writes on the back, with a shaking hand, this last
prayer. "These were the last lines she wrote on earth."

NOTES

At first sight somewhat convoluted, and thus surprising on the part
of Thérèse, this prayer has been considered a pastiche of words commonly
attributed to St. Augustine: "Lord, my soul rejoices greatly
when it thinks that you are God, for if the impossible could be that Augustine were God and you were Augustine, I would prefer it better that you
had been God and not Augustine." This saying is included in R. P.

Ribadeneira, *Vie des Saints at fêtes de toute l'année* [Lives of the Saints and Feasts of the Year], trans. by M. l'Abbé Daras, 3rd ed. (Paris: L. Vivès, 1862), month of August, p. 489. It was the custom in Thérèse's time to read these *Lives of the Saints* in the refectory. Saint Francis de Sales repeats the same saying with a few variations in his *Treatise on the Love of God.* "Well, Lord, I am Augustine and you are God; but if however, which neither is nor can be, I were God and you were Augustine, I would want, by changing qualities with you, to become Augustine so that you might be God." (*Oeuvres de Saint François de Sales, Traité de l'Amour de Dieu*, vol. 1, Book V, chap. VI, p. 277). Let us note the gloss: "by changing qualities with you" which well sums up the intention of this Pri 21. In May 1897, to define Mary's attitude towards us, her total detachment on our behalf, Thérèse had sung: "To love is to give everything. It's to give oneself" (PN 54.22). A few days before her death, she made this need her own, on Mary's behalf, in a sentiment of mutuality that implies an exchange of identity.

Biblical Index of the Prayers

N.B. The column at the left indicates the biblical chapter and verse, the column at the right, the number of the prayer and the line.

OLD TESTAMENT

Exodus 17:9–13	8,20–23	Canticle 2:16	5.cover; 5v.9
		Canticle 4:6	6.69
1 Kings 19:10.14	17.1; 18v.2–3	Canticle 5:2	12v.4–6
Judith 13:7	17.4–5		
		Wisdom 3:5–6	6.39–40
Psalms 23[24]:7–9	20.19	Wisdom 3:6	6.1–2
Psalms 30[31]:21	12r.1		
Psalms 83[84]:7	8.43–44; 9.11	Isaiah 53:3	12v.8–9, 11, 29–30
Psalms 89[90]:4	6.53	Isaiah 64:6	6.49
Psalms 89[90]:5	7.5		
Psalms 90[91]:4	5v.7		
Psalms 136[137]:1–4	12v .23–26		
Canticle 1:1	16.8		

NEW TESTAMENT

Matthew 9:1	27.13–14	John 13:8	20.36
Matthew 10:34	17.2	John 13:15–17	20.7–9
Matthew 11:29	5r.3; 20.2, 10–11, 25, 47	John 14:2	6.10
		John 14:2–3	2.19
Matthew 18:19–20	9.1–5	John 16:23	6.28–29; 13.1–3
Matthew 24:30	6.41	John 17:15	8.26
Matthew 25:6	5r.1	John 19:28	12v .14–15
		John 20:27	6.42
Luke 2:51	20.15–16		
Luke 7:42–43	7.16–17	1 Corinthians 1:27	17.17
Luke 14:10	20.28, 35	1 Corinthians 3:12	6.71; 17.31
Luke 14:11	20.31–34		
Luke 23:9, 11	3.3–4	Galatians 6:17	6.42
John 3:16	6.14–15; 13.5–12	Philippians 2:7	20.4–5, 18
John 7:37	6.56–57	Hebrews 5:7	6.27
John 12:26	17.25–27		
John 13:5	20.5	Revelation 7:9	18r.1–2
		Revelation 14:4	13.30–33

The Institute of Carmelite Studies promotes research and publication in the field of Carmelite spirituality. Its members are Discalced Carmelites, part of a Roman Catholic community—friars, nuns, and laity—who are heirs to the teaching and way of life of Teresa of Jesus and John of the Cross, men and women dedicated to contemplation and to ministry in the church and the world. Information concerning their way of life is available through local diocesan Vocation Offices, or from the Vocation Director's Office, 1525 Carmel Road, Hubertus, WI, 53033.